The Chess Pub Quiz Puzzle Book

Dimitri Reinderman

The Chess Pub Quiz Puzzle Book

Who is MC Hammer and other Chess Trivia

New In Chess 2023

© 2023 New In Chess

Published by New In Chess, Alkmaar, The Netherlands
www.newinchess.com

Cover design: Buro Blikgoed
Supervision: Delia Keetman
Editing, typesetting: Sandra Keetman
Proofreading: Delia Keetman
Production: Sandra Keetman

Have you found any errors in this book?
Please send your remarks to editors@newinchess.com. We will collect all relevant corrections on the Errata page of our website www.newinchess. com and implement them in a possible next edition.

ISBN: 978-94-93257-79-5

Contents

Preface

My quiz career started somewhere in 1995. I was active on Usenet (newsgroups, a precursor of internet forums) and saw people sharing lyrics quizzes. 'I can do that too!', I thought, and I did: over a period of about four years, I made sixteen quizzes, with more than a hundred people in total participating. But, like in chess, engines became a problem. More and more answers were searchable, and I stopped making quizzes.

In the new century, I found out about pop (music) quizzes in real life. The concept is simple: the quiz master plays fragments of songs, and you must write down (with your team) the artist and title of the songs. As it turned out, I was good at that. I played occasionally at first, a few times a year, but as I got to know more people and learned about more quizzes, it became a big part of my social life. Currently I play about six quizzes (both pub (trivia) and pop) per month.

Just like with the lyrics quizzes, I wanted to make pop quizzes myself, but it took some time before I could host my own quiz. May 22, 2011 was the day, and it was both a fiasco and a success. It was hosted in a bar that used to have monthly pop quizzes, but they had enough of it, and mine would be the last. Unfortunately, this meant that they didn't bother to generate any publicity for it. Only eighteen people showed up, most of whom I had invited myself. But they all had a great time, which encouraged me to go on with it. And so my quiz-making career was started. Ever since, I have hosted many pop quizzes, not only in bars, but also as side events of the Open and the closed Dutch Championships.

Word got around and I was also asked to make and host chess trivia quizzes, for example by New In Chess as a Christmas event. This was a bigger challenge. Making a pop quiz is easy: think of a theme, for example kings and queens, find titles and artists that fit the theme (often a matter of CTRL-F) and make a good selection. The chess quiz was hard work, but it was received well, or at least I was asked again by New In Chess. And maybe this led their managing director Remmelt Otten to think: if this is fun in real life, it might be fun on paper too! So, he asked me to make a chess pub quiz book.

What does it take for a quiz/puzzle to be fun? The questions shouldn't be too easy, but certainly not too difficult either. If you know all the answers without any effort, it doesn't give you satisfaction. If you hardly know any answers, it's demotivating. My goal was to make the puzzles solvable, but with some effort. Different people will have different areas of expertise in chess trivia, just like in chess. That is why there are a few ways to make finding the answers to the questions easier if necessary. Many of the puzzles come with an acrostic (explained on the next page), giving you letters for the answers. There are also hints for some puzzles at the end of the book, which you can use if you get stuck. And probably it is easier (and more fun?) if you try to solve the puzzles together with someone else. You can even enjoy parts of this book together with a non-chess playing friend or partner, since not all the puzzles require chess knowledge.

For me (and probably for others too), apart from the challenge of solving, there is another thing that I enjoy in quizzes: you learn new facts. That is the second goal of this book: to enable you to learn something new. To add to this enjoyment, I borrowed something from a Dutch quiz show called *Per Seconde Wijzer* ('wijzer' means both 'wiser' and 'hand of a clock'). There, each round is introduced with a little fun fact story. I did the same in this book. Hope you find at least some of them interesting!

Dimitri Reinderman
January 2023

Explanations of the puzzles:

Acrostic

A lot of puzzles in this book include an acrostic. In an acrostic, letters correspond to the same numbers in the solution and in different answers. Finding the word(s) of the solution can help you to solve the puzzle. Below you can find an example of this.

1. The player to move has no legal move but is not in check.
2. A move in which the king and rook are moved at the same time.
3. The family name of grandmaster Teimour.

1	S^5	T	A^2	L^4	E	M	A^2	T	E^6
2	^{1} A^2	S^5		L^4		^{7}	
3	^{3} A^2			A^2			

Solution:

The answer to question 1 (stalemate) is already filled in. The S corresponds with 5, the fifth letter of the solution. The same goes for the A (2), L (4) etc. In answer two, again 2, 5 and 4 are used. So now you already know three letters of the answer: A, S and L. And if you find the solution, you get two letters more.

A simpler version is used in a few puzzles in which each answer gives just one letter of the solution (already in the right order).

Matching the answers and questions

In some puzzles, the answers are already given, but they must be matched with the right questions. In the example below, you see the names of three chess players. The task is to match them with their countries.

The countries to choose from: Egypt, Norway, the Netherlands

Player	Country
Anish Giri	
Magnus Carlsen	
Samy Shoker	

You might not know from which country Samy Shoker is. But if you match Giri with the Netherlands and Carlsen with Norway, there is one answer left: Egypt. And indeed, Shoker is an Egyptian grandmaster.

Photo Connection

There are five Photo Connection puzzles. Here you will see 27 pictures, divided into three blocks: pictures 1-9, pictures A-I and pictures R-Z. You must find three pictures that match, one from each block. A simple example:

The queen in 1 matches with B (the band Queen) and Z (Queen Elizabeth). The king in 2 matches with A (the king of the jungle) and Y (Martin Luther King). So, the solution is 1-B-Z, 2-A-Y.

What's the connection?

In the 'What's the connection?' puzzle, there are ten questions. The answers to the first nine questions have a (chess-related) connection. Question 10 is then: who or what connects the answers to the above questions? A simple example:
1. Who wrote *The Hustler*, *The Color of Money* and *The Man Who Fell to Earth*?
2. Which actress with the first name Anya played in movies like *Last Night in Soho*, *The Menu* and *Amsterdam*?
3. Which streaming service was founded in 1997 in California and is now one of the biggest in the world?
4. Who or what connects the answers to the above questions?

The answers are 1. Walter Tevis (who wrote *The Queen's Gambit*), 2. Anya-Taylor Joy (who played the main character in *The Queen's Gambit*) and 3. Netflix (the streaming service that released *The Queen's Gambit*). So, the answer to question 4 is, you guessed it, *The Queen's Gambit*.

Some other things

In the time between us making this book and you reading it, things may have happened that render certain questions and/or answers incorrect/outdated, like players changing nationalities/federations. Please answer those questions with the end of 2022 in mind.

Some players have names that are not always spelled the same, e.g., Yusupov/Jussupow, Ding Liren/Liren Ding. In general, here we use the same spelling as in the Chessbase Playerbase. For the acrostics, the exact spelling of a name can be important. If you are unsure (for example about the first name of Duda, or whether Ding or Liren is the surname), you can look it up. This book is not meant as a spelling test.

Talking about looking things up: there is no arbiter, so you can make your own rules. But I do hope that your primary rule is: to have fun!

Guess the moves

The move 23...♛g3 from the game Levitsky-Marshall is often in the top three in lists of the best or most fantastic moves ever played. It is certainly impressive, but was it necessary? Computer says no. Black is a piece up, and moving the queen to another square (a3, b4, b2, even e3) would have won too. What about the story that the board was showered with gold coins after the move, is that true? Well, Marshall himself has confirmed it is. However, his wife later denied the story: 'Coins there were, yes – but gold coins, narry a one!' It has been suggested that the coins were a payment. Another hypothesis is that enthusiastic spectators collected (gold) coins for Marshall and presented them to him after the game. Or maybe both are true, and Marshall combined them to make a nice story?

The diagrams on the next two pages feature twelve other legendary positions. Do you know what moves were played? And who were the players? The games are in chronological order.

	Players	Moves		Players	Moves
1			7		
2			8		
3			9		
4			10		
5			11		
6			12		

Hints on page 119
Solution on page 121

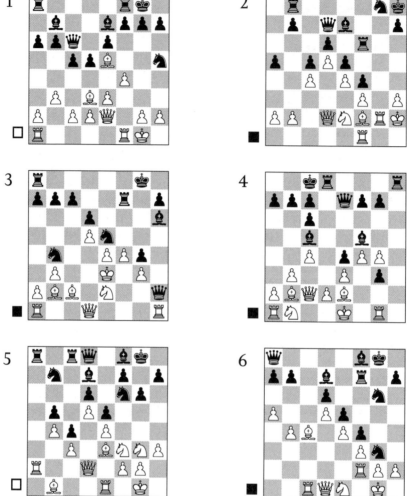

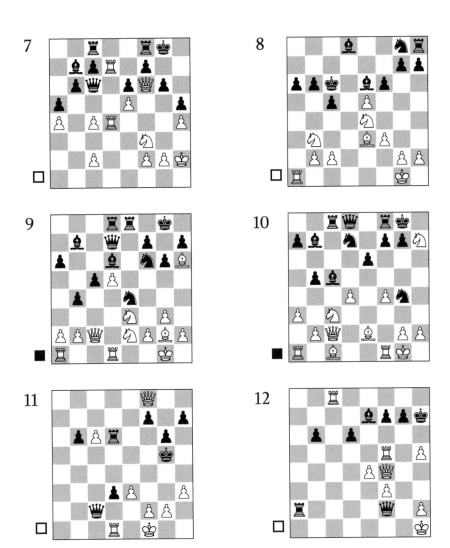

7

8

9

10

11

12

When they were young 1

In 1944, World Champion Alexander Alekhine barely managed to make a draw against his pupil, a 13-year-old prodigy named Arturo Pomar. The Spanish boy became famous in his own country, but later didn't quite fulfil his early promise: chessmetrics.com has as his highest rank #23 in the world. Still, he became the Spanish champion seven times, and became Spain's first grandmaster in 1962.

In the pictures you see 12 boys that did fulfil their early promise. What are their names?

1	(first letter surname)
2	(first letter given name)
3	(last letter surname)
4	(first letter given name)
5	(last letter surname)
6	(first letter surname)
7	(last letter surname)
8	(first letter given name)
9	(last letter surname)
10	(first letter given name)
11	(last letter surname)
12	(last letter surname)

Solution:

1	2	3	4	5	6	7	8	9	10	11	12

Hints on page 119
Solution on page 122

Fair & Square 1: grandmasters

A well-known quote is 'Play the opening like a book, the middle game like a magician, and the endgame like a machine.' It is attributed to Rudolf Spielmann, but is it really his? According to chesshistory.com, the quote is much older: it was already written in an 1896 book by Mason and Pollock, where it was attributed to 'a great player'. Whoever that is, it was not Spielmann: he was 13 at the time.

The attribution of quotes is not always easy! I hope you know the nine quotes given below. To make it easier, the nine persons are already given: you only have to match them with the right quote.

1. '(Chess) doesn't feel like working. Of course, it's how I earn money, but I just think about it as a way to have fun. Sometimes, it feels as though it's my life. Especially at tournaments. The whole atmosphere. The excitement. I find myself thinking "This is where I want to be". It draws me in!'

2. 'Chess is the most creative, fascinating and challenging game there is; and the most exciting, spine-tingling form of chess is Blitz.'

3. 'Like all lunatics I am convinced that the doctors here are madder than I am.'

4. 'I claim like 1% responsibility for the current horrible situation in world chess, because I did write a short memo to Kramnik before the Kramnik-Kasparov match, "The Berlin is quite playable." '

5. 'In fact, I am quite surprised that I managed to achieve quite a lot in chess, because I am not a sportsman inside. I don't care so much about competing, I don't care about being the best (...) I am really an artist in my attitude.'

6. 'I never in my life tried coffee... I basically also never in my life tried beer.'

7. 'What's this? Are you teaching the poor thing to play chess? Fie, for shame! Why not have him drink hard liquor or take him off to a brothel, while you're at it!'

8. 'Women use less plans, less logical thinking and tend to rely on concrete move-by-move play.'

9. 'You have a chance to become a good chess player if you travel to play chess, not play chess to travel.'

Person	Quote
Hein Donner	
Ivan Sokolov	
Magnus Carlsen	
Peter Leko	
Peter Svidler	
Sergey Tiviakov	
Vladimir Kramnik	
Walter Browne	
Wilhelm Steinitz	

Solution on page 122

Chess players and their eyes

Since 1961, Olympiads have been held for blind and visually impaired players. In the third of these, in Weymouth 1968, the organisers experienced some unforeseen difficulties: the Polish team arrived with a dead body, their sighted guide. The organisers had to move the body to the mortuary and find a Polish speaker in the seaside resort who would be willing to spend two weeks to help the Polish chess team. What are the odds? But he found one! Poland finished 12th out of 20 teams.

In the pictures, you see the eyes of fourteen sighted chess players. Each name will give you a letter, the letters will make a word.

1	(last letter surname)
2	(last letter given name)
3	(first letter surname)
4	(last letter surname)
5	(first letter surname)
6	(first letter surname)
7	(first letter surname)
8	(first letter surname)
9	(last letter surname)
10	(first letter surname)
11	(first letter given name)
12	(last letter surname)
13	(first letter surname)
14	(first letter surname)

Solution:

1	2	3	4	5	6	7	8	9	10	11	12	13	14

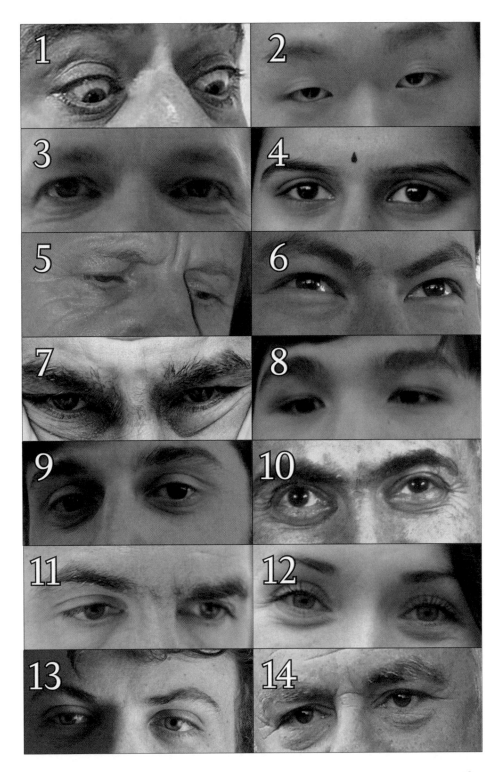

Hints on page 119
Solution on page 122

19

What's the connection? 1

Some non-Dutch chess players assume that Wijk aan Zee is a big city, since it is so famous in the chess world. It is a small village with a population of about 2175. I have been told that during summer there are even more tourists than inhabitants in Wijk aan Zee. That also explains why the Tata Steel Tournament is organised in winter: the village has lots of (otherwise) unused hotel beds at that time of the year.

Your knowledge of this tournament, and more, is tested in the next questions.

1		(6,6)
2		(5,8)
3		(6)
4		(3,7)
5		(4)
6		(7)
7		(3)
8		(5,4)
9		(4)
10		(5,5)

1. What is the name of the 1945 children's novel by E.B. White, in which the main character is as small as and looks exactly like a mouse? In 1999 the book was adapted into an animated movie with the same name.

2. Who is the only player who won the Wijk aan Zee tournament three times in a row?

3. In which city were the 2004 Summer Olympics held?

4. Which electronic dance music band is led by Liam Howlett?

5. In which year did the following events happen? The second Kashmir war between India and Pakistan, the release of Like a Rolling Stone by Bob Dylan, Spassky beating Keres, the assassination of Malcolm X, and Geller and Tal winning Candidates matches.

6. What is the lingua franca of chess?

7. MDMA (3,4-Methylenedioxymethamphetamine) is commonly known as which three-letter word?

8. Which chess term has been described by Tim Krabbé as follows: 'It has to be on the fifth rank at least, and when it has reached that rank, the opponent must have at least three pieces left (four, if we include his king) and one of them has to be a queen. Also, the game must be won by the player who has it.'

9. What is the name of the 2018 biopic of Dick Cheney?

10. Who or what connects the answers to the above questions?

Hints on page 119
Solution on page 123

Photo Connection: countries

Wikipedia has a list of openings that were named after countries. I thought I was quite familiar with offbeat lines, but there was so much on the list I didn't know! What is 1.d4 f5 2.e4 fxe4 3.♘d2 ? American Gambit. And 1.e4 c6 2.d4 d5 3.♘c3 dxe4 4.♘xe4 h6 ? Finnish Variation. What about 1.f4 f5 2.e4 ? Swiss Gambit. Even stranger: 1.d4 ♘c6 2.d5 ♘b8 3.e4 ♘f6 4.e5 ♘g8, the Zaire Defence.

The openings in diagram 1 to 9 are also named after countries, but they are less obscure. Do you know them, and can you link them to pictures A-I and R-Z?

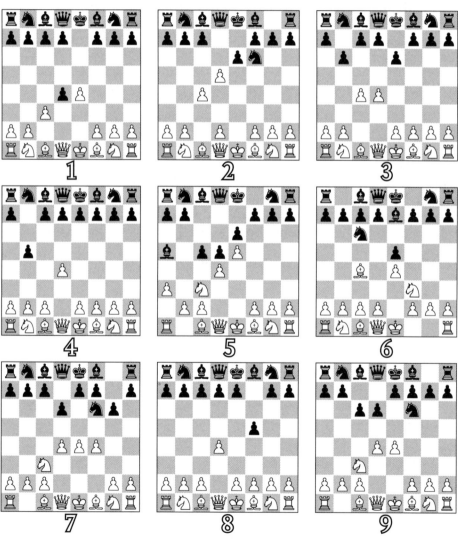

	A-I	R-Z		A-I	R-Z		A-I	R-Z
1			4			7		
2			5			8		
3			6			9		

Solution on page 123

Anagrams

In an open tournament in Kottayam (India), a player entered the under 1400 section as an unrated named Shripati Jana. After 8 rounds, he had 7.5 points, and the organisers were suspicious, even after Jana produced an election card as proof of his identity. Fortunately, they knew an arbiter with a very good memory. They sent him a picture of Jana via WhatsApp, and their suspicions were confirmed: the arbiter recognized the player and told the officials his real name. They confronted the cheater, who confessed.

Your task is similar. Fifteen names of well-known chess players have been scrambled. What are their real names?

1. Alarming pic

2. Ashamed claim

3. Cleanest favours

4. Daredevil if moves

5. Hiring piano vandals

6. I ate, drank, ask no luxe

7. I give risk a vote

8. Ignorant pirates

9. Joint keeper

10. English Rot (aka Longer shit)

11. Mini tinder admirer

12. Self boarding

13. Slow eyes

14. Thwarted males

15. Undo vail bid

1	6		3		2				9					
2		9			3			3				5		
3					8		3		–					
		7	2				1							
4			3		9				–					
				7	8									
5	4	7	10		11		6	2			–			
		3	5											
6	3					10		2		–				
			8			4	9							
7	5		2	11			1						7	
8	1		11		3		–							
	6		1			8								
9			2	7		4	6	9			1			
10	10		11			5		7		1				
11		9		9	1	2	9	–						
	2		9	4			2		3	10				
12			2	9	8						4			
13			8				5	7						
14		3	1	1				8					2	
15		3	10	9	9					7				

Solution:

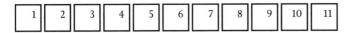

1	2	3	4	5	6	7	8	9	10	11

Hints on page 119
Solution on page 123

Guess the blunders

In 1916, Isidor Gunsberg sued the *Evening News* for libel. They had written that his chess columns contained blunders. He won 250 pounds for damages to his reputation: the British High Court ruled that oversights are not blunders. So, for safety reasons, the twelve diagrams below are given without names. Solve this puzzle at your own risk! Who made the blu... ehm, oversights, and with which move?

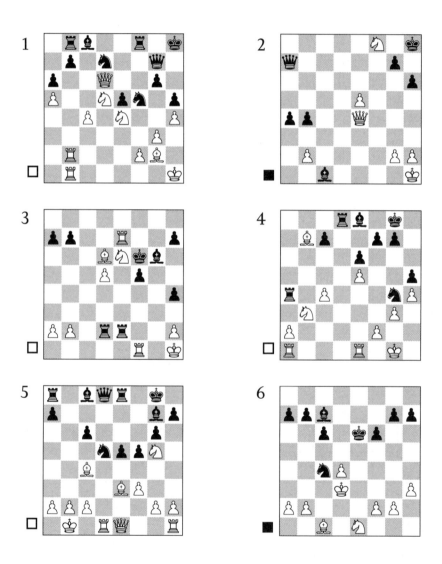

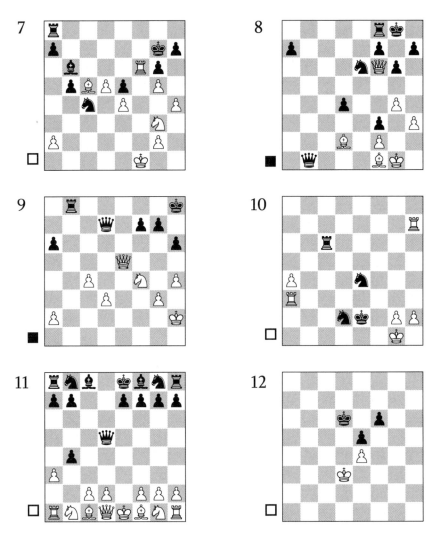

	Player	Blunder		Player	Blunder
1			7		
2			8		
3			9		
4			10		
5			11		
6			12		

Solution on page 123

Celeb64: movies

The 1925 Soviet comedy *Shakhmatnaya Goryachka* (*Chess Fever*) combines footages of the Moscow 1925 tournament with acting. Several famous chess players are in the movie as a cameo. The role of a chess-hating World Champion is played by Capablanca, making him one of the strongest chess-playing actors ever. You can find *Chess Fever* on YouTube with English subs. Talking about movie celebs from the past, do you recognize the fifteen in the pictures?

1 ☐ 10 10 ☐ 8 12 ☐ ☐ 7 ☐

2 ☐ 7 10 ☐ ☐ 6 ☐ ☐ ☐ 3 ☐ 8

3 ☐ 10 ☐ ☐ 3 ☐ ☐ 8 —

☐ ☐ 10 10 ☐ ☐ 8

4 12 ☐ ☐ 11 ☐ 13 ☐ ☐ ☐ 13

5 ☐ ☐ ☐ ☐ 8 ☐ ☐ ☐ ☐ 14 10

6 3 ☐ 6 ☐ 7 ☐ 7 —

☐ ☐ ☐ 14 6 ☐ ☐ 1

7 ☐ 5 ☐ 13 ☐ ☐ 8 14 ☐ 3 4 ☐ ☐

8 ☐ ☐ 8 ☐ ☐ 2 ☐ ☐ ☐ ☐ 8

9 ☐ 12 3 ☐ ☐ ☐ 7 12 ☐

10 4 ☐ 14 ☐ 6 ☐ 12 ☐ ☐

11 ☐ ☐ ☐ 8 11 ☐ ☐ ☐ 14

12 ☐ ☐ 14 1 ☐ 13 ☐ ☐ 7 —

☐ ☐ ☐ 7 2 ☐ 7

13 ☐ 14 ☐ ☐ ☐ 3 ☐ ☐ 2 ☐ ☐ ☐

14 9 ☐ 9 9 8 ☐ 12 6 ☐ ☐

15 ☐ 14 ☐ ☐ ☐ 7 8 ☐ 2 9 13 ☐ ☐ ☐

Solution:

1	2	3	4	5	6	7	8	9	10	11	12	13	14

Solution on page 124

Ranking the stars: 2000s Olympiads

The 44th official Chess Olympiad was held in 2022. In all those Olympiads the player who scored the most points is Lajos Portisch: 176.5 out of 260 games. The highest percentage among players with at least 30 games is by Mikhail Tal: 82/101 is 81.2%. In the Women's Olympiads, Maia Chiburdanidze scored the most points: 125.5/167. That is 75.4%, a high percentage, but it's not even close to Alla Kushnir's 23/25 which makes 92%!

All these stats, and much more, can be found on the site olimpbase.org. This is the work of one man, Wojciech Bartelski. Unfortunately, the site hasn't been updated in recent years, but it's still impressive!

Since 2000, there have been eleven Olympiads. Twelve countries scored at least one medal in the Open and/or Women sections. Can you guess which ones? 1 2 3 (6) means the country scored one gold, two silver and three bronze medals, six in total.

1. 7 4 1 (12)

2. 5 5 4 (14)

3. 4 3 5 (12)

4. 3 1 2 (6)

5. 1 2 3 (6)

6. 1 2 2 (5)

7. 1 0 0 (1)

8. 0 2 0 (2)

9. 0 1 1 (2)

10. 0 1 1 (2)

11. 0 1 0 (1)

12. 0 0 3 (3)

1	1				6				
2					7				
3				6		4			
4	6				5				
5			6						
6		3				7			
7				3					5
8	2		4						
9	7			6					
10				6	5				
11		3				4			
12	7				6				

Solution:

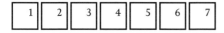

1	2	3	4	5	6	7

What's in a name? 1

Does luck exist in chess? In 2003, Alexander Huzman played Garry Kasparov (who he had lost to in a clock simul five years earlier) with White. He was outplayed in the opening and after 20...♖e8 (preparing 21...♗c8) Black would have been clearly better. However, Kasparov blundered with 20...♗c8??, missing 21.♖xd5!. After 21...♕e8 22.♗xc4, the boss resigned. And Huzman? He is forever known as the man who scored an upset win against Kasparov.

In this task, twelve more players who made their marks in history are described. What are their names?

1. Siamese Cats + alcohol

2. Big Al + beat nine world champions

3. Think Like a Grandmaster

4. Chess Queen + 2008-2010 Women's world champion

5. The Yerminator

6. Time trouble addict + 3x World blitz champion

7. WW2 cracking Enigma + 2x British champion

8. Coach of Kasparov

9. Revived Albin Countergambit + 3x winner Biel

10. Born in Brazil + lives in Georgia

11. 1999 World Champion

12. Women's World Championship Challenger in 1975 and 1981

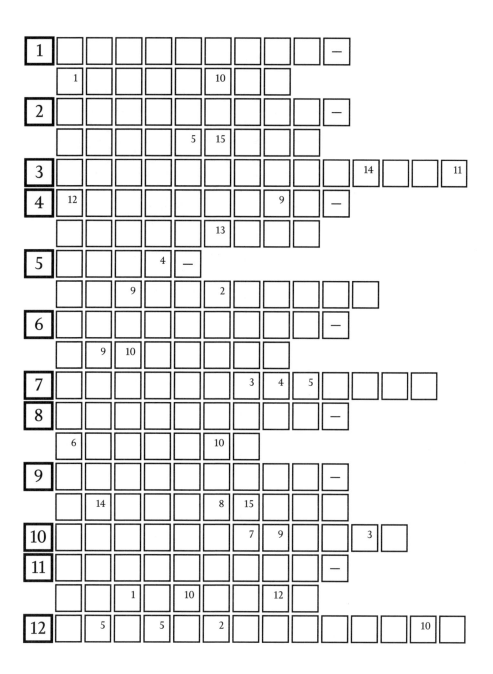

Solution on page 125

When they were young 2

One of the biggest stunts in chess tournament history is what became known as 'the sack of Rome': Sofia Polgar scoring 8.5/9 in an open tournament in Rome in 1989 with a tournament performance of around 2900. It was one of the best performances ever, and she was only 14 years old at the time, rated 2295. She would be a professional player for more than 20 years, but she never made it to the top. Later, Sofia switched careers and currently she is an artist and illustrator. The girls in the pictures are also very talented. What are their full names? For No. 6, the family name is enough.

1	4				9		2		8		11
2	3				2	6		5	—		
			12	15		16					
3	14	13		14	13	14					
4		18		18		18	—				
		2					8	17	18		
5		5		5	10		5	1			10		16
6		11		9		4					
7		6			14		6	11		4	
8	3		12	8					18	—	
	1				18						
9	16	13				7			4	—	
		5		4							
10		14			6	15			12		1		2
11	10				17		13	13		—	
	4				14						
12	4	2		9			18				

Solution:

1	2	3	4	5	6	—

7	8	9	10	11	12	13	14	15	16	17	18

Hints on page 119
Solution on page 125

Timeline of chess history

The earliest chess machines (automatons) were hoaxes and were operated by people from inside the machine. Peter Hill was one of those operators, hidden in a machine called Ajeeb. It was not without danger though. When the machine beat a woman player, she stabbed Ajeeb with a hatpin, wounding Hill (who remained quiet). On another occasion, a Westerner emptied his six-shooter into the automaton. Hill fortunately survived. Ajeeb was not the first automaton: that was The Turk. But when was it built? And when did the other 11 events below happen? To help you, the years are given, you just have to link them to the right event.

1. Adolf Anderssen wins the first international chess tournament in London.

2. Alekhine dies as the reigning World Champion.

3. Alexander McDonnell of Ireland and Louis-Charles Mahé de La Bourdonnais play a series of six matches.

4. Baron Wolfgang von Kempelen builds the Mechanical Turk, a fake chess-playing humanoid 'machine' in fact operated secretly by a human.

5. Establishment of the Fédération Internationale des Échecs (FIDE), the international chess federation.

6. FIDE introduces the titles International Grandmaster and International Master.

7. François-André Danican Philidor born in Dreux, France.

8. Hungary wins the first official Chess Olympiad in London.

Vera Menchik becomes the first Women's World Champion.
9. Mechanical game clocks are introduced in tournament play.

10. Paul Morphy travels to Europe and easily beats the leading players there.

11. Steinitz becomes the first World Chess Champion.

12. The first edition of the book *Neue theoretisch-praktische Anweisung zum Schachspiel* by Johann Allgaier is published.

Year	Event	Year	Event
1726		1883	
1769		1886	
1795		1924	
1834		1927	
1851		1946	
1858		1950	

Solution on page 125

Wikipedia

Wikipedia only has two principles: articles should be neutral, and everyone can edit them. These principles are sometimes difficult to unite, for example in pages about politically sensitive subjects. Such pages are semi-protected, to prevent anonymous and newly registered users from editing them.

This has happened also to the Wikipedia page about chess. There are some controversies, and it is also not allowed to call chess a sport, much to the chagrin of some.

Still, Wikipedia is a great source of information about chess players. The twelve descriptions on the next two pages are copied from Wikipedia. You only need to fill in their surnames.

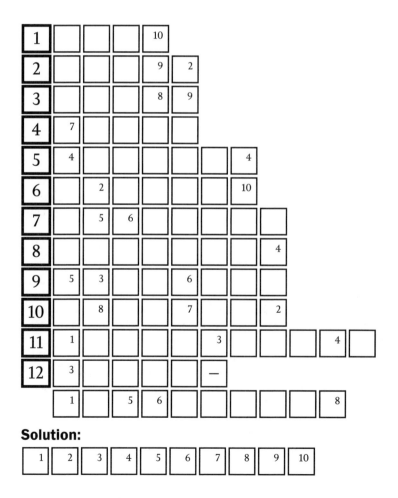

Solution:

1. …. was undefeated in classical chess from August 2017 to November 2018, recording 29 victories and 71 draws. This 100-game unbeaten streak was the longest in top-level chess history, until Magnus Carlsen surpassed it in 2019.

2. ….. claims to be 'the author of 140 books on chess'. He was the Chess Advisor to Batsford. […] In 1989, he and Nathan Divinsky wrote *Warriors of the Mind*, an attempt to determine the 64 best chess players of all time. The statistical methods used have not met with wide approval, but the player biographies and games were regarded by one book as providing a good overview but also incurred criticism for inaccuracy. Much of ….'s later work has attracted criticism for sloppiness, plagiarism and the habit of copying passages, including errors, from one book to another.

3. …..'s creative style was greatly influenced by Chigorin and Alekhine. He was a highly intuitive, natural player. He was considered to be a brilliant attacking genius, but nevertheless played very sound chess, being less willing than Tal to complicate with unforeseeable results. […] He was one of few players who had an even score against Vasily Smyslov, Tigran Petrosian, and Mikhail Botvinnik. He had plus records against Mikhail Tal, Boris Spassky, and Paul Keres.

4. ….. has the distinction of being the first Asian player to earn the title of International Grandmaster. He qualified for the Candidates Matches for the 1984 World Championship. In that preliminary stage, the contenders play matches against each other to determine who will challenge the world champion. ….. was eliminated when he lost his match against Zoltán Ribli by a score of 6–4.

5. ….. was born in the town of Tuapse, on the shores of the Black Sea. His father's birth name was Boris Sokolov, but he took his stepfather's surname when his mother (…….'s grandmother) remarried. His mother Irina Fedorovna is Ukrainian and is a music teacher; his father is a painter and sculptor. As a child, ……. studied in the chess school established by Mikhail Botvinnik.

6. ……. was a chess prodigy, drawing comparisons to Bobby Fischer, although he did not achieve the International Grandmaster title until 1972. He won the Interzonals of Petropolis 1973 and Manila 1976. His highest FIDE rating is 2635, achieved in 1977, when he was ranked number four in the world. He became the 3rd best in the world in 1977, behind only World Champion Anatoly Karpov and Viktor Kortchnoi.

7. …….. began playing chess at age three. Throughout her childhood, both of her parents were actively competing at chess. When she was young, she typically accompanied her parents to chess tournaments because her only regular babysitter was her maternal grandfather, who was not regularly available to babysit because he lived in Sweden.

8. At the end of 2017, …….. gained widespread media attention for her decision to boycott the World Rapid and Blitz Championships in Saudi Arabia and forgo the opportunity to defend both of her World Championship titles because of the restrictions Saudi Arabia has in place against women, including those related to women's clothing and the incapability of women to go outside without being accompanied by a man.

9. A former child prodigy, he earned the title of Grandmaster in March 2001 at the age of 14, making him the second youngest grandmaster in history at the time. In 2003, …….. gained international attention after beating the then world No. 1 Garry Kasparov in the Linares tournament, followed by victories over former world champions Viswanathan Anand and Ruslan Ponomariov all in the same year.

10. …….. earned the IM title at the 1998 African Zonal (zone 4.3) with the required 66% score and later went on to win the first of his two African Junior Championships in 1999 by 12/13 followed by an 11/11 score in 2000 during which he earned the moniker 'The Zambezi Shark' and became famous for repeatedly defeating his competition in Fischer-like fashion, winning tournaments by large margins.

11. To celebrate ………..'s 60th birthday, a Sicilian Defence-themed tournament was held in recognition of his contributions to the opening. The event was funded by Luis Rentero and took place in Buenos Aires in October 1994. ……….. was too ill to participate.

12. At the Chess World Cup 2017, where …………… was organizer, he berated player Anton Kovalyov for wearing shorts, racially abusing him with the slur 'gypsy' and demanding that Kovalyov change ten minutes before his scheduled third-round game, leading to Kovalyov withdrawing from the tournament in response. …………… received heavy backlash from the global chess community for this incident, including a condemnation from the Association of Chess Professionals and calls from other players demanding that he be removed from his organization roles.

Chess players with a beard and/or a moustache

In April 2017, IM Aman Hambleton, one of the Chessbrah streamers, shared with everyone that he had decided not to shave until he would be a grandmaster (for fun and as motivation). He scored his second GM-norm that month but didn't play as well in following tournaments. Meanwhile his beard grew bigger and bigger... fortunately, he made his last norm in December. Finally, he could shave! But he was happy with his challenge: 'In the end it did its job, and it made a lot of people follow me on my journey to GM so it turned out to be great publicity.'

Do you recognize these sixteen other chess players with a beard and/or a moustache?

1	(last letter surname)
2	(last letter given name)
3	(first letter given name)
4	(first letter given name)
5	(first letter surname)
6	(last letter surname)
7	(first letter surname)
8	(first letter given name)
9	(last letter surname)
10	(first letter given name)
11	(last letter surname)
12	(first letter given name)
13	(first letter surname)
14	(first letter given name)
15	(last letter surname)
16	(last letter surname)

Solution:

1	2	3	4	5	6	7	8	—

9	10	11	12	13	14	15	16

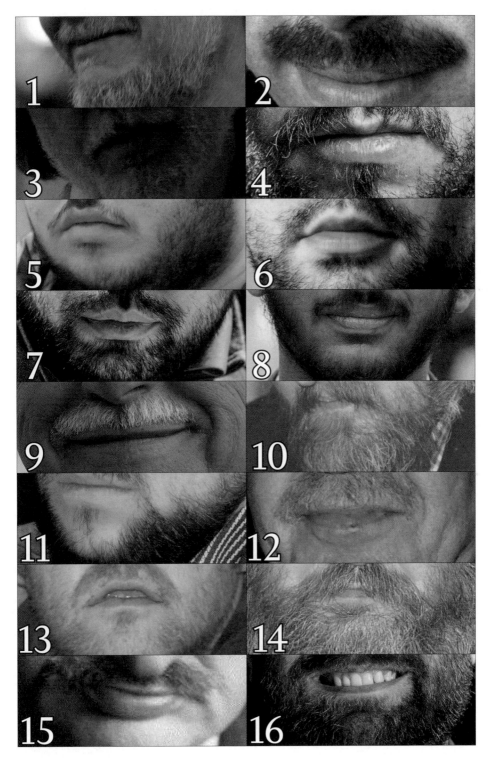

What's the connection? 2

What tournament is sometimes described as The Wimbledon of Chess? This is a bad quiz question, as it has two answers. If you answer Wijk aan Zee/Tata Steel, you are correct. However, the Linares tournament, which was held from 1978 to 2010, also had this nickname. Especially in the nineties, this tournament was really an elite event, with the 1994 edition even having the highest average rating ever at the time.

This is not the only connection between Wimbledon and chess. For example, there is a chess pub quiz book that includes a question about Wimbledon.

#		
1		(5,6)
2		(7,1)
3		(4,4)
4		(9)
5		(9)
6		(5,7)
7		(8)
8		(5)
9		(4)
10		(4,9)

1. Who is the youngest Wimbledon gentlemen's single champion?

2. Which British rock band has had hits like *So Long*, *The Worker* and *Marliese?*

3. What is a business called that offers secured loans to people, with items of personal property used as collateral?

4. What is the world's northernmost capital of an independent state?

5. In duplicate bridge, players sometimes do a deliberate bid of a contract that they are unlikely to make, in the hope that the penalty points will be less than the points the opponents would gain by making their contract. What is the term used for this?

6. Which actor played the main character in *Spider-Man* (2002) and the sequels 2, 3 and *No Way Home?*

7. What is the title of the 1970 hit song that starts with the lines 'Finished with my woman, 'cause she couldn't help me with my mind. People think I'm insane, because I am frowning all the time.'

8. What is the title of the 2006 movie about the assassination of U.S. Senator Robert Kennedy?

9. In what year was the author of this book born?

10. Who or what connects the answers to the above questions?

Hints on page 119
Solution on page 126

Photo Connection: political leaders

Which grandmaster has had the highest position in politics? Kasparov intended to run for president but withdrew due to obstruction. Karpov is just a member of the parliament. Reizniece-Ozola has been Minister of finance and of economics, but she's not a GM but a WGM. Stefanova is a GM with a successful political career, but I think the answer is Čmilytė-Nielsen. She was the leader of the opposition in Lithuania in 2019. This is nowhere near the power the men in pictures 1 to 9 have. How do they connect to pictures A-I and R-Z?

	A-I	R-Z		A-I	R-Z		A-I	R-Z
1			4			7		
2			5			8		
3			6			9		

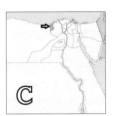

World Champions

World Championship matches have often seen incidents. You probably know about the yoghurt incident and Toiletgate, but have you heard about Adjourngate? It was during the 29th game of the 1935 match Alekhine vs Euwe. After Euwe (with Black) played his 40th move, Alekhine, instead of writing down an adjourned move, played his 41st move on the board! Perfectly legal, but unusual, and evidently not done according to the members of the organising committee, who asked the arbiter to object to the World Champion's action. Euwe was wiser – he told the committee members not to disturb him and sat down to think about his adjourned move.

Euwe would become the 5th World Champion, with Steinitz being the first and Kasparov the 13th. Below you find descriptions of the first thirteen World Champions. Your task it to fill in the right surname for each description (and transfer the right letter to the solution box corresponding with the question).

1		(1st letter)
2		(3rd)
3		(2nd)
4		(7th)
5		(3rd)
6		(2nd)
7		(3rd)
8		(1st)
9		(3rd)
10		(4th)
11		(1st)
12		(3rd)
13		(6th)

1. The briefest World Champion.

2. A professor in computer science.

3. Born in Finland.

4. In *From Russia with Love*, James Bond played a game based on his game against Bronstein.

5. Married four times.

6. Named after President Truman.

7. He won 185 international tournaments.

8. The first to become World Champion in his birthplace.

9. He played at Candidates' level 46 years apart.

10. The son of Paul Felix Nemenyi.

11. He died as a Soviet citizen in the USA.

12. He died at age 64, but not in Iceland.

13. He wore a hearing aid.

Solution:

1	2	3	4	5	6	7	8	9	10	11	12	13

Solution on page 126

Chess books

The second book ever published in English was *The Game and Playe of the Chesse* by William Claxton in the 1470s. The book does not tell you how to play chess, but is an allegory. The first real chess book is the Göttingen manuscript, published in Latin around 1500. Since then, many more chess books have been published. Can you recognise them by the covers? Just the title is enough.

Solution:

1	2	3	4	5	6	7	8	9	10	11	12

Solution on page 127

Fair & Square 2: singers, actors and writers

When chess is mentioned in a movie or a television series, it is often not accurate, to say the least. This can be funny, but often it's a bit annoying. One of my favourite chess scenes is in the Dutch comedy series *Toen was geluk heel gewoon* (literally, 'When happiness was quite common'). In the 1997-episode *Chess*, sewer worker Simon Stokvis (!) turns out to be a strong chess player. He beats the boss of his best friend and stuns the viewers with the explanation of his win: 'After that queen exchange, my plus pawn becomes more important as castling has blocked your rook – which, anyway, in the Sicilian defence can't do much against my Grünfeld-Indian middle game. It's just like the sixth game from the sensational chess match between Dr. Lasker and Capablanca in Havana 1921, when Dr. Lasker opted, with a piece sacrifice, for a draw by perpetual check, but he had overlooked the bishop on f8 which he only noticed when the flag fell. Yeah, then Capablanca was, of course, world champion.'

The following nine quotes are less impressive. The nine persons who uttered them are already given in the table on the right, but who said what?

1. 'Chess-players are so unsociable; they are no company for any but themselves.'

2. 'From the time homo ludens crawled from the primeval slime of spillikins and strip checkers and first called himself a man, the 64 squares and 32 pieces that define limits of chess have exerted a powerful fascination over the species.'

3. 'I failed to make the chess team because of my height.'

4. 'I look at improvising as a prolonged game of chess. There's an opening gambit with your pawn in a complex game I have with one character, and lots of side games with other characters, and another game with myself – and in each game you make all these tiny, tiny moves that get you to the endgame.'

5. 'I love Rita, she's great. We ended up playing a game of chess. There was a board in one of the rooms, and we were like, "Let's go". It was a half-a**ed game, but she won.'

6. 'I would certainly end up forever crying the blues into a coffee cup in a park for old men playing chess or silly games of some sort.'

7. 'Marriage is like a game of chess except the board is flowing water, the pieces are made of smoke and no move you make will have any effect on the outcome.'

8. 'When it came to the actual chess sequences, my background as a dancer really helped – it's basically just choreography with your fingers.'

9. 'When I was 18, science, physics, and maths were my favourite. I was a bit of a nerd – the only girl with a lot of boys at chess championships.'

Person	Quote
Anne Brontë	
Anya Taylor-Joy	
Björk	
Charles Bukowski	
Charli XCX	
Jerry Seinfeld	
Stephen Fry	
Steve Carell	
Woody Allen	

Solution on page 127

Celeb64: movies and TV

There are (at least in the Netherlands) a lot of television shows in which celebrities learn a certain skill. Dancing, diving, ice skating, pottery, photography, boxing, curling, you name it. We have almost everything except chess. I guess the television program creators don't find chess interesting enough, but as you can see in the pictures, celebrities do! Who are they?

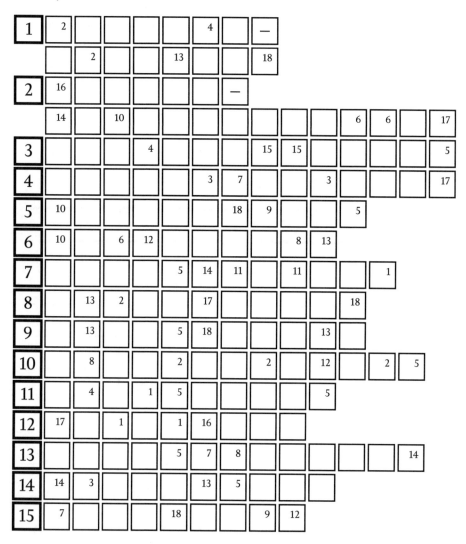

Solution:

1	2	3	4	5	6	7	8	9	10	—

11	12	13	14	15	16	17	18

Solution on *page* 127

Nicknames

In the strong 1903 Monaco tournament, Richard Teichmann (1868-1925) finished in 5th place, a decent result for him. In the same year, in the Vienna Gambit tournament, he finished shared 5th again. Nothing special, but when he finished 5th in Hamburg 1905 and (shared) in Ostend 1905, a pattern was discovered. Vienna 1908, Prague 1908, Hamburg 1910 (shared), all fifth places. And so, he got his nickname 'Richard the Fifth'. He actually had won a lot of tournaments too, but those were neglected. Teichmann was not the only player who was nicknamed for his tournament results, but probably Walter Browne (1949-2015), aka Mr. Six-Time, was happier. He won the US Championship six times!

Below you find seventeen nicknames of chess players. Most of them are given, some are self-chosen. Can you give the real (sur)names?

1. Ale and Wine

2. Chess Buccaneer

3. Chucky

4. DrDrunkenstein

5. GingerGM

6. J'adoubovic

7. Minister of Defense

8. PenguinGM1

9. The Artist

10. The Boss

11. The Good Doctor

12. The Great Dane

13. The Human Chess Machine

14. The Patriarch

15. The Professor

16. The Tiger of Madras

17. The Walking ECO

A number grid puzzle. Each numbered row contains cells, some marked with numbers.

#										
1	10			1	14					
2		2	16		8	11				
3		9				14	3	7		
4	13		4		17					
5		6			6			16		
6				3		2			13	
7	1		4				6			
8		10	5							
9		6	4							
10	7		17				8	9		
11		3		5						
12		10		16	15					
13	13			10				5		10
14		11		9	6				1	
15		2				14		9	17	7	
16		5		5						
17	12	3			10	5				

Solution:

1	2	3	4	5	6	7	8	9	10	—

11	12	13	14	15	16	17

Solution on page 127

When they were young 3

Do you know in which year China first participated in the Olympiad? You might know about the Chinese Immortal, the game Liu Wenzhe-Donner in the 1978 Olympiad, but there were no previous participations. At the start of the Cultural Revolution in 1966, chess was forbidden in China, and the ban was lifted only in 1974. One year later, the Malaysian business tycoon Dato Chin Nam started the 'Big Dragon Project' with the goal to have China dominate the chess world in 2010. And even though it didn't quite succeed, there are many strong players from China and other Asian countries now. Can you recognize these twelve players born in Asia from their youth pictures?

#													
1	11		10			5	9				1			8
2	6			5				6			1			
3		2			6		3		13					
4	9				3			10	—					
	12			5	4		7	7		3				
5			3		1		3			13	13		2	
6	7				8	4			11					
7	7		1		3		12	3						
8		2			8			9						
9			4	6			4							
10	12		2				12	—						
		2					12							
11				10				13	—					
		8		11				13						
12			5	10			11							

Solution:

1	2	3	4	5	6	7	8	9	10	11	12	13

Hints on page 119
Solution on page 128

Players who represented at least three federations

The story of Paul Keres and his nationalities is just as tragic as that of his country. When he was born in 1916, Estonia was a province of the Russian Empire. In 1918, Estonia became independent. The annexation by the Soviet Union happened in 1940, in 1941 the Germans occupied Estonia and made it part of Ostland. In 1944, Estonia again became part of the Soviet Union. Keres tried to escape to the West, but failed, and for the rest of his life he was a Soviet citizen.

Fortunately, nowadays when a player changes his or her (chess) nationality, it's their own doing. Some even do it more than once. Can you find the twelve grandmasters that represented at least three countries? Just the surname is enough.

1. Armenia, Germany, USA

2. Chile, Netherlands, Spain

3. France, Monaco, Switzerland

4. Latvia, Germany, Azerbaijan

5. Ukraine, Spain, Turkey

6. USSR, Belgium, Turkey

7. USSR, Israel, USA

8. USSR, Georgia, Czech Republic, Slovakia, Armenia

9. USSR, Latvia, Bangladesh, Czech Republic

10. USSR, Russia, Germany, Belgium

11. USSR, Russia, Israel, Switzerland

12. Yugoslavia, Bosnia and Herzegovina, Netherlands

Solution:

1	2	3	4	5	6	7	8	9	10	11	12	13

Solution on page 128

Photo Connection: pop music

Of all the pop songs in which chess is mentioned, my favourite is *Cue Fanfare* by Prefab Sprout, though I don't understand the lyrics:

When Bobby Fischer's plane
Plane, plane touches the ground
Plane, plane he'll take those Russian boys
And play them out of town,
Playing for blood as grandmasters should.

Check it out! But first, try to recognize the pop artists in picture 1 to 9 and link them to the pictures A-I and R-Z.

	A-I	R-Z		A-I	R-Z		A-I	R-Z
1			4			7		
2			5			8		
3			6			9		

What's the connection? 3

The common octopus (*octopus vulgaris*) is an intelligent animal. It has 500 million neurons in its body, almost comparable to a dog, and can navigate mazes, recognize individual people and learn to unscrew a jar or raid lobster traps. It has three hearts and can change colours like a chameleon, not only to blend in with the surroundings, but presumably also to communicate with congeners. And it can even communicate with people to predict football matches... well, maybe.

1		(4)
2		(4,5,9)
3		(7,9)
4		(3,10)
5		(6,6)
6		(9,3,5)
7		(3,4)
8		(7,5)
9		(3,11)
10		(4,4)

1. What was the name of the octopus that achieved worldwide fame by giving accurate predictions of football matches in the 2010 World Cup?

2 The song *Suspicious Minds* became a big hit by Elvis Presley. Which band had a hit with it in 1986?

3. Who won the 1990 Nobel Peace Prize for the leading role he played in the radical changes in East-West relations?

4. Which Formula One driver has been dating Kelly Piquet (the daughter of Nelson) since October 2020?

5. Who is the composer of *Adagio for Strings* (1936)?

6. Which Macedonian king created an empire from Greece to north-western India?

7. What is the capital (and largest city) of Costa Rica?

8. Which Ivorian international played for among others, Feyenoord, Chelsea, Lille and Hertha BSC?

9. Which country has the tallest people based on average height?

10. Who or what connects the answers to the above questions?

Hints on page 119
Solution on page 129

Breaking the rules

Cheating is a hot topic in chess, but it is not a recent phenomenon. In *Life at Play*, the memoir of Lubomir Kavalek, the Czech/American grandmaster gives several examples of players who didn't abide by the rules. One opponent was singing each time when it was Kavalek's turn to move. Other opponents discussed variations with friends during play. And in some tournaments, opponents or even organisers expected him to lose a game in exchange for money. None of these villains were sanctioned. Below you find ten examples of (alleged) foul play. Can you link them to the names of ten perpetrators? To protect their privacy, only the first letter of their last name is given.

1. As a dreadlocked, headphone wearing, unrated newcomer he scored 4.5/9 in the open section of the 1993 World Open. When quizzed by the tournament director, he was unable to demonstrate even basic knowledge of chess and he got disqualified.

2. Falsified tournament reports to gain the GM title and a 2635 rating in 2001. He avoided sanctions by his national federation by becoming their president. FIDE decided he had to prove his rating in a tournament selected by FIDE. His score was 0.5 out of 9. Eventually his title and high rating were quietly removed.

3. He bragged in Facebook chats about manipulating results in a 2017 tournament he had organised and played in. However, the manipulation was not proved. A federal court did suspend him for 5 months from competitive play for shameful behaviour in public and private statements. GM Igor N. was suspended for six months for offering to lose a game in exchange for money in the same tournament.

4. He defeated Gothamchess in an online 10-minute game with suspicious time usage. Gothamchess checked his games, saw an over 90% accuracy and reported the account, which was blocked by chess.com. His son made the case public and Gothamchess received many hate messages. A sponsor organised an $21,000 match between him and Irene Sukandar. He lost 3-0, making many basic mistakes. He did win about $7,000 for losing.

5. He scored 6.5 out of 9 at the 2010 Olympiad, which was good for a gold medal. According to his federation, this was done with computer assistance: the team coach would position himself in the hall behind one of the other players' tables in a predefined coded system, where each table represented a move to play. He and his

coach got sanctioned by the federation, but those were revoked by a court. In 2019 he was sentenced by a court to a suspended sentence of 6 months in prison for the cheating accident.

6. His daughter told him she heard player X ask, 'How's the evaluation?' in the ladies room. He made it public on an internet forum, adding that the rating of X had increased from 2177 to 2420 in five months, and giving some examples of suspicious moves in her games. After a complaint from X and her parents, he was sanctioned by the FIDE ethics commission for making unsubstantiated allegations of cheating. In an open letter, 41 grandmasters supported him.

7. In a tough rook endgame, while his opponent Hans Niemann was thinking, he picks up his opponent's king on b3 and twiddles with it. The cross falls of. He throws the king back at square b6. The game continues and Niemann wins.

8. In 1980, he set up a computer assistance scheme as a test. He told an amateur who was playing a GM in a simul secretly the moves that the chess computer Belle would play. The amateur won (from a lost position). The GM hadn't noticed anything unusual.

9. In the finals of the 2020 Pro Chess League he beat So, who publicly accused him of cheating. He replied with 'You are the biggest loser I have ever seen in my life' and other insults. Chess. com investigated his games, deprived his team (who had won the finals) of the victory and banned him for life.

10. In 2012 in a Bundesliga game he took (according to his opponent) a second toilet break already at move 10 (which he denied later). On his return, an arbiter asked him to hand over his phone. He refused and was forfeited the game. His federation issued a two-year suspension, but after an appeal the arbitration court of the federation cancelled the ban.

Person	Description	Person	Description
Alexandru C.		John von N.	
Dadang S.		Pier Luigi B.	
Evgeniy S.		Samuel S.	
Falko B.		Sebastien F.	
Frederic F.		Tigran P.	

Solution on page 128

Chess players with glasses

My favourite 'Weird Al' Yankovic song is *White and Nerdy*, and not only because I can relate ;). He raps about typical interests of nerds: 'I'm nerdy in the extreme and whiter than sour cream, I was in AV club and Glee club and even the chess team!' Indeed, chess is often seen as a hobby for nerds. And what does a nerd look like? He or she wears glasses. The sixteen people in the pictures have all been in the chess team, who are they?

#												
1	8				6			1				
2		2						—				
	8						5					
3	11			11					9			12
4			9	9			15				4	
5				6		6	4	—				
					6							
6		3						4				3
7			10		10							
8	3			4			1					
9		3		11		13						
10		14			14		14					
11		2			12		12	—				
	11		12			7						
12	4				9	8				4		
13	3			8	7							
14		1	15					1				
15	5			12	3		10			12		
16				14	7	13			11			

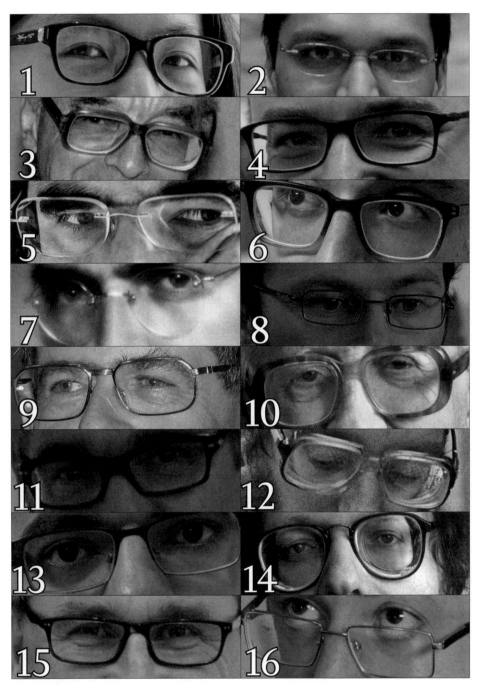

Solution:

1	2	3	4	5	6	7	8	9	10	11	12	13	14	15

Solution on page 129

Two descriptions

In the 1963 World Chess Championship Match, Tigran Petrosian beat Mikhail Botvinnik. In the 1998 U16 Olympiad, again Tigran Petrosian beat Mikhail Botvinnik. Of course, these were different people which happened to have the same names as the former World Champions. The new Tigran was named after the famous World Champion and would later become a strong grandmaster himself. In the next 14 questions, you get two chances to find the right answer. If you don't know what or who the first description is about, you still can get the right answer by knowing the second one!

#	Grid
1	1
2	2
3	9 2 3
4	4
5	5
6	6 7
7	8 10
8	10
9	11
10	10 12
11	13 13
12	14
13	14 7
14	15 15 15

Solution:

1	2	3	4	5	6	7	8	9	10	11	12	13	14	15

1. It is the name of the beloved cat of Alekhine that was stolen during the 1935 Olympiad in Warsaw. It is also the name of the record company of artists like Muddy Waters, Chuck Berry and Howlin' Wolf.

2. It is the Italian and Spanish word for rook. It is also the surname of a North American player who got awarded the grandmaster title in 1977 at age 72.

3. It is the name of the first wife of Siegbert Tarrasch. It is also a chess player with the nickname Miss Strategy.

4. It is the surname of a grandmaster who was sentenced in 2019 by a French court to a suspended sentence of 6 months in prison for his actions in the 2010 Olympiad. Change the first letter and it is the surname of the grandmaster whose moves 11.♘xe6 fxe6 12.♕h5+ ♔f8 13.♗b5 were copied on two adjoining boards in Gothenburg 1955.

5. It is the title of a big hit by Katy Perry and Juicy J. With an article added, it is the title of a 2014 New Zealand movie about a chess player.

6. It is the name of the supercomputer that gave the answer to the ultimate question of life, the universe, and everything. It is also the name of the winner of the 1989 World Computer Chess Championship.

7. It is the surname of the father of Leon Trotsky. It is also the surname of the first person to be the youngest grandmaster in the world.

8. It is the name of the gambit 1.e4 e5 2.♗c4 ♗c5 3.d4. It is also the name of the 12th century chessmen found in 1831 on a Scottish isle.

9. It is the name of a 1971 song by Elton John. It is also the given name of the winner of the 2017 edition of Norway Chess.

10. It is the name of the opening 1.f4 f5 2.e4. It is also a way to avoid being paired with strong opposition in a tournament.

11. It is the name of the youngest and most famous daughter of the last Russian Tsar, Nicholas II. It is also the name of a certain mate with knight and rook, for example ♘e7 and ♖h5 against ♔h7 and pawn g7.

12. It is the most common surname in France. It is also the surname of an English IM, author of many opening books and DVD's.

13. It is the team's name of Magnus Carlsen and Jon-Ludvig Hammer when they won the 2019 Reykjavik chess pub quiz. It is also the name of a rapper that had hits like Pray and 2 Legit 2 Quit.

14. It is the name of a pairing system in chess. It is also the name of a Sicilian variation.

Solution on page 129

What's in a name? 2

Long before Carlsen, there was a Northern European player who was hailed as a potential World Champion. In 1977, he won the first official under-17 World Championship, ahead of later giants like Kasparov and Short. In the same year he became Icelandic champion for the first time. Alas, after that he developed slowly, and he only became a grandmaster in 1986. Around 1995 he stopped playing competitively and started a successful career in business and finance. Did you guess who it is? It is Jón Árnason.

Below you find twelve even shorter descriptions. Who are they about?

1. The best of the west

2. Ended Carlsen's unbeaten streak

3. The Fed

4. The challenger + difficult name

5. gmjlh

6. New in Chess

7. 3x British champion – Big glasses

8. co-founder chess24 – Jan's Opening Clinic

9. Grandmaster at age 62 – Latvia

10. 3x Slovak champion – Under the Surface

11. PhD in mathematics – Beating the Sicilian

12. Estonian American – The Story of a Chess Player

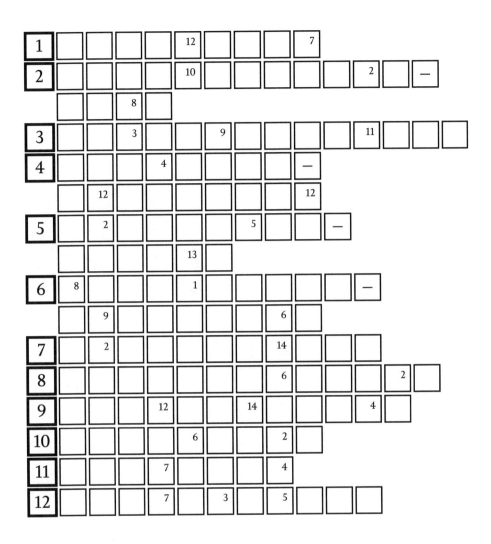

Solution:

1	2	3	4	5	6	7	8	9	10	11	12	13	14

Solution on page 130

Logos

The word logo is short for logotype. Logos means word, type means symbol. So, a logo is a word symbol, a symbol representing a word (or more words). Some logos have one or more words in them. Maybe that's why nowadays we don't call them logotypes but just logos. In these sixteen pictures, you see the symbol (a logo or part of a logo), you name the word(s) they represent.

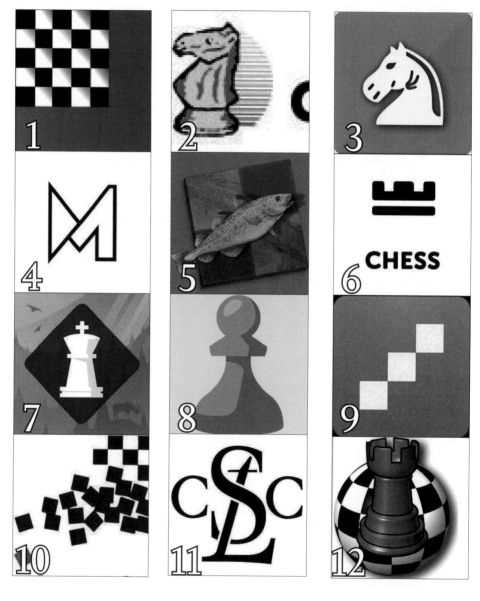

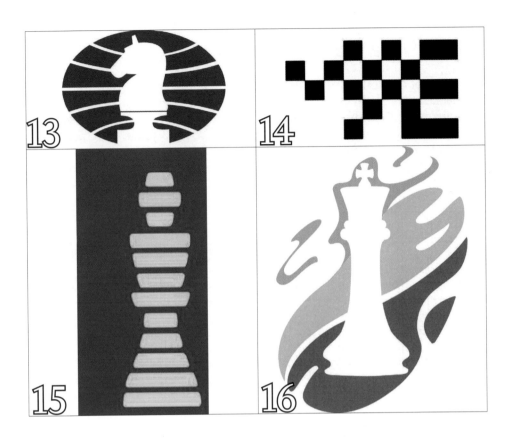

1		9	
2		10	
3		11	
4		12	
5		13	
6		14	
7		15	
8		16	

73

Hints on page 120
Solution on page 130

When they were young 4

The trend of the top grandmasters becoming younger and younger is especially visible in Wijk aan Zee. In 1985, the average age of the participants in Grandmaster group A was about 33. Twenty years later (with Carlsen playing in the B-group) it was about 30 years. The Tata Steel Masters in 2023 had an average age of about 25. That means that most of the boys in the pictures (born 1990 or later) would have been considered old there! What are their names?

1 | 5 | | | 4 | 5 | | — |

| | 1 | | 3 | 4 | | 14 | | | | 14 | | | |

2 | 14 | | | 6 | 14 | | 14 | 6 | | | | 14 | |

3 | | | 7 | — |

| 7 | | | 10 | | 11 | | | 13 | | | 13 | 11 |

4 | | 15 | | | 14 | | 8 | 12 | | | | | — |

| | 9 | | 15 |

5 | | | 7 | | 9 | | | | | — |

| 3 | | 5 | 5 | | 14 |

6 | | | 14 | | | 7 | — |

| | 1 | 7 | | | 14 | | | 12 | |

7 | | 5 | 4 | | | 8 | — |

| 6 | | | | | 4 | | 4 | 7 |

8 | | 15 | 2 | | | | | | 15 | | | | | 15 |

9 | 13 | | | 12 | 7 | | | 10 | | | 7 |

10 | 1 | | | | 3 | | | | 11 |

11 | 6 | | 8 | 6 | | | 6 | | 4 |

12 | | 15 | | 11 | | 13 | | | | | |

Solution:

1	2	3	4	5	6	7	8	9	10	11	12	13	14	15

Hints on page 120
Solution on page 130

Twelve cities

World Championship matches are usually played in big cities. Not all of them were, though – there has been a game that was played in a town with a population of less than 10,000. It is a famous game: Game 26 of the Alekhine-Euwe match in 1935, labeled the 'Pearl of Zandvoort'! By winning this game, the challenger took a two-point lead with four games to go and that turned out to be enough to win the match. The twelve cities described below are quite a bit bigger than Zandvoort. Can you name them?

1. Everyone knows that the World Championship Match between Spassky and Fischer in 1972 was held in Reykjavik. However, originally this match was supposed to be hosted in two cities. In which city was the first half of the match scheduled to be played?

2. In 1889 and 1892, Steinitz and Chigorin played a World Championship Match in a city in which Lasker would also play a WC match. Which one?

3. In which city was the immortal game Andersen-Kieseritzky played?

4. In which foreign city did the Russian player Alexander Ilyin-Genevsky live for a while, winning the city championship in 1914?

5. Normally, there is no connection between the Olympiad and the Summer Olympics, but there has been one exception. In 1928, both events were held at the same time and in the same country. Which city hosted the 1928 Olympiad?

6. The first three World Champions all died in the same city. Which one?

7. The first World Championship chess-boxing was held in 2003 between Iepe Rubingh (winner) and Jean Louis Veenstra. The author of this book was one of the support acts. In which city was this?

8. What is the capital of Kalmykia, which features Chess City?

9. Which city has a popular variation named after it in both the Sicilian and the Slav Defence?

10. Which city organised both a World Championship match and an Olympiad in the 21st century?

11. Which city will be the host of the 2024 Olympiad? It was also the host of the second unofficial Olympiad in 1926.

12. Wikipedia has a list of grandmasters including (if known) their birthplace. According to this list, which city (outside of Russia) is the birthplace of the most grandmasters?

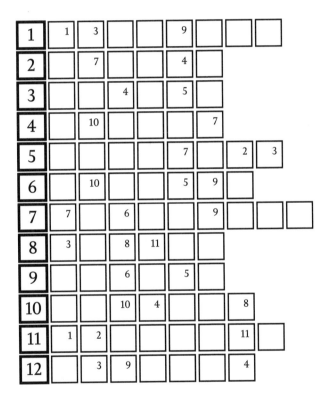

Solution:

Solution on page 131

Celeb64: music

The first solo album of Peter Hammill (lead singer of the progressive rock band Van der Graaf Generator) is called *Fool's Mate*. You might think with such a name that he is a beginner in chess, but no. When Bert van de Kamp (1947-2020, he worked for New In Chess in the eighties, but was better known as a leading pop journalist in the Netherlands) had to interview Hammill for the Dutch music magazine *Oor* ('ear' in English), they decided to play chess. Van de Kamp extensively analysed the game in the article he later wrote, and both turned out to be very decent club players. It's unlikely that most of the other celebs in the pictures have that level...

1				5	2				9	7			18					
2	14	11	11	10		19		16	16					2				
3		15			4	17		3	3			6	10	20				
4	8				15		9					11						
5		1	13	2		5	17	14										
6		1			4		7	11										
7		19	15			15	—											
		13			12					15		13						
8	6	13			3		11		12	12								
9	16							5		16								
10			4	—														
11	7	2			20	18					3	3						
12			9		4	&		13	20									
13		12		11														
14				12	15			15			20	16						
15		1		1														

Solution:

1	2	3	4	5	6	7	8	9	—
10	11	12	13	14	15	16	17	18	19	20

Solution on *page 131*

Who?

One of the most prominent chess historians is Edward Winter. He started a bimonthly periodical called *Chess Notes* in 1982, and since 2004 these chess notes have their own site, chesshistory.com. Each chess note is numbered and has one topic. There is one title that comes back in a lot of chess notes: 'Who?' with the content being an unnamed photograph of a chess player. This puzzle is a tribute!

In the acrostic, surnames are enough.

1. In 2001, less than two months before his 80th birthday, Victor Kortchnoi beat a 2721 rated player with the black pieces. Who was this player?

2. Which famous singer had a crush on Bobby Fischer (a year younger than her) when she was 16?

3. Who is the highest rated 60+ grandmaster?

4. Which chess writer won all four major Book of the Year awards: English Chess Federation (2010), ChessCafe.com (2001), Association of Chess Professionals (2013) and the Boleslavsky Medal from FIDE's trainer committee (2012)?

5. Of all the grandmasters, dead or alive, who was born the earliest?

6. Who was the first African chess player to receive the grandmaster title?

7. Which player has withdrawn twice from a Candidates match, both times a point down?

8. The first official rating list came out in July 1971. Which grandmaster, born 20-9-1896, was in last place with a 2170 rating?

9. The federation with the best score at the Olympiad Open and Women's section combined gets a trophy. Whom is this trophy named after?

10. From 1985 to 1993, Victor Kortchnoi played a correspondence game. His opponent was a medium called Robert Rollans, who claimed to get the moves from a strong master who lived from 1870 to 1951. Who is this master?

11. Which grandmaster was from 2004 to 2014 in a relationship with the Estonian supermodel Carmen Kass?

12. Which three-time Women's World Championship Challenger left chess in 1978 to become a world-renowned archaeologist and a professor in Tel Aviv?

13. Who is the only twofold (2003 and 2005) Junior World Champion?

14. Who was the first player to win the World Championship in a double round-robin tournament?

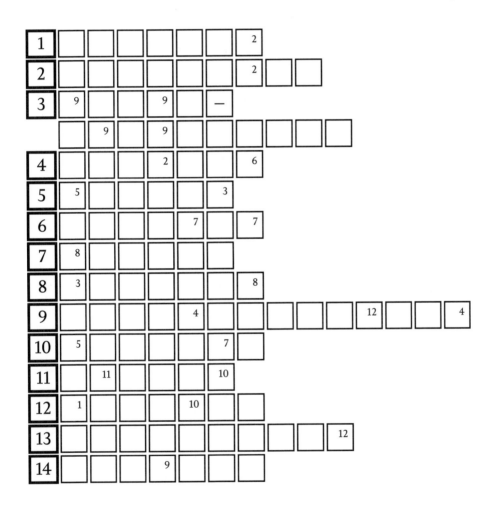

Solution:

1	2	3	4	5	6	7	8	9	10	11	12

Solution on page 131

Photos: TV series

From 1976 to 1983, the BBC broadcasted a show called *The Master Game*. It was a televised knockout tournament with top grandmasters like Karpov, Larsen, Nunn and Short. Each episode was about half an hour and featured one game being shown on an innovative display board accompanied with the thoughts of the players (recorded after the game) in a voice-over. A great format which I wish would still exist. A few episodes can be seen on YouTube, for example the game Short vs Byrne.

Fortunately, in regular TV series they also play chess occasionally. Twelve famous series can be seen in the pictures. What are the titles?

1				2	10						
2	8						6				
3	3				8		9				
4		4			7						
5	3					2					
6	5				2						
7	3						4			10		
—			1			—	6				
8	3										
9		2		10		2					
10		6	8					2			
11	3			9				2			
12	8				7		5			9		

Solution:

1	2	3	4	5	6	7	8	9	10

82

Solution on page 131

Interviews from New In Chess

Dirk Jan ten Geuzendam has been tournament director, team captain at the Olympiad, commentary host at tournaments and chess columnist for a Dutch newspaper, but you probably know him best because of his work for New In Chess. Below you find quotes of nine interviews by him (and one by Jonathan Tisdall). Who were the interviewees?

1. 'At some point, I had this social media company that was handling my social media accounts, but it didn't quite work out. Also, because they messed a few things up and posted things which weren't quite true or which were just flat-out mistakes. Like once they said my favourite song was *Kashmir* (by Led Zeppelin), but they spelled it *Cashmere*. And then I got so many messages telling me how it should be spelled.'

2. 'The amount of classical music I listened to when I was mourning was tremendous. And Bach always comes to the rescue, of course. He is there at any moment, on any occasion. More than anything else, I listened to his works for violin, for piano, for solo instruments. They are closer to me than his oratorios.'

3. 'Kamsky told me, you should play like yourself no matter what the tournament standings are. You should just try to win, because that's who you are. [...] That was something that Kamsky made me realize, and it really helped me at the Olympiad.'

4. 'I feel attracted to these worlds of fiction, because I really want to experience much more than my own life. I don't really think that my life is interesting enough, and by watching or reading or playing all this, no matter if it's fantasy or based on real life, I get to know more stories, which fulfils my life.'

5. 'I have literally had organizers write to me and say we'd love to invite you, but we already had too many US players. I look forward to more such emails. But at the end of the day, look, Aronian didn't break any rules, so I can disagree with the rules all I want, but as long as someone's following them you can't blame him.'

6. 'I have this habit of drinking tea to keep some energy during the game. And it stops you from hasty decisions, which is nice. You want to make a move, but first you open the thermos, you pour the tea, you put it back and then you start thinking. It's part

of the ritual. When I was seven years old, I was told by Soviet coaches to sit on my hands. This is another solution.'

7. 'I saw this book by Wim Hof, you know, *The Iceman*, which had good reviews. At some point he says, if you really want to feel well, and this has been demonstrated scientifically, you have to start taking cold showers. It's great for your heart, for your stress levels, for your blood vessels. [...] And so I started taking cold showers on Day 1 in Wijk aan Zee, the day of my arrival. This became a huge ritual as the tournament progressed. I started with half a minute, then built it up to one minute. He says you should do this five of the seven days in the week, but I did it every day. After this cold shower I felt great and full of energy for the rest of the day. The toughest part was behind me.'

8. 'I understand that you may not believe this, but I was very glad after the tournament. I knew I had done good work in my preparation, and I played well. OK, so it happened that I didn't win. If I had won on top of all of this, that would have been fantastic, but it was enough for me to be happy. Everybody around me was feeling, what a pity, you played so well, but frankly I myself didn't feel like this at all.'

9. 'My biggest advantage is that I am better in chess.'

10. 'When I was a kid, chess looked like a brilliant world to me. I wanted to be Morozevich or Svidler. I mean, I wanted to play brilliant games like Shirov. I wanted to have a smart face like Kramnik. They all gave interesting interviews. They were not afraid to speak. [...] Now, when I see, for instance, Anish and Magnus on Twitter, I mean, they're like kids.'

Person	Quote	Person	Quote
Daniil Dubov		Magnus Carlsen	
Fabiano Caruana		Sam Shankland	
Gukesh D		Vladimir Kramnik	
Jorden van Foreest		Wang Hao	
Levon Aronian		Yan Nepomniachtchi	

Solution on page 131

Fair & Square 3: politicians and others

In Wijk aan Zee they understand that a good relationship with policy makers is important. Every year Tata Steel Chess organises a simul for members of the Dutch parliament with a grandmaster from the Masters group. Senator Loek van Wely hasn't participated himself, though he probably did give some advice to participating fellow party members. During Tata Steel there is also the Dutch Championship for (former and current) parliamentarians. A regular participant is Jan Nagel, often successfully. Not strange, since he is the father-in-law of Yasser Seirawan!

They are not in the list below, but five other politicians are. Can you link them and the four others in the list with the right quote?

1. 'Chess is a fantastic game, it teaches rules and discipline, it is a very logical game, it directs the energy of children in a certain direction, otherwise they might start making mischief, it makes sense to encourage them to deal with chess, it's the biggest puzzle game ever invented.'

2. 'Chess is an example of something that is just beyond human mental abilities, but not so far beyond them that we cannot make a decent stab at it. We're very good at language, no better than rats at mazes, and somewhere in between at chess.'

3. 'Chess is a simple game. Understandable when all we had to play with were squirrels and rocks, but now we have computers.'

4. 'Daring ideas are like chessmen moved forward. They may be beaten, but they may start a winning game.'

5. 'If you look at the democratic process as a game of chess, there have to be many, many moves before you get to checkmate. And simply because you do not make any checkmate in three moves does not mean it is stalemate. There's a vast difference between no checkmate and stalemate. This is what the democratic process is.'

6. 'It's all a very, very beautiful game of chess, or game of poker, or – I can't use the word checkers because it's far greater than any checkers game that I've ever seen – but it's a very beautiful mosaic.'

7. 'It's always difficult to play a double game: declaring a fight against terrorists while simultaneously trying to use some of

them to arrange the pieces on the Middle East chess board in one's interests.'

8. 'There is a big difference between a calculated risk and a foolish gamble. Business is like a giant game of chess: you have to make strategic moves and learn quickly from your mistakes.'

Person	Quote
Arnold Schwarzenegger	
Aung San Suu Kyi	
Boris Johnson	
Donald Trump	
Elon Musk	
Johann Wolfgang von Goethe	
Noam Chomsky	
Richard Branson	
Vladimir Putin	

Solution on page 132

Photo Connection: sport

You might have heard of chess-boxing, which is an official sport. In the Netherlands we have tournaments with football, running, tennis or snooker combined with chess. My favourite is 'schafeltennis' (chable tennis), in which a match consists of four games of table tennis and two games of blitz chess. Among the participants have been grandmasters like Loek van Wely, Robin Swinkels and me. The nine athletes in picture 1 to 9 excel in just one sport. Do you recognize them, and can you link them to the pictures A-I and R-Z?

	A-I	R-Z		A-I	R-Z		A-I	R-Z
1			4			7		
2			5			8		
3			6			9		

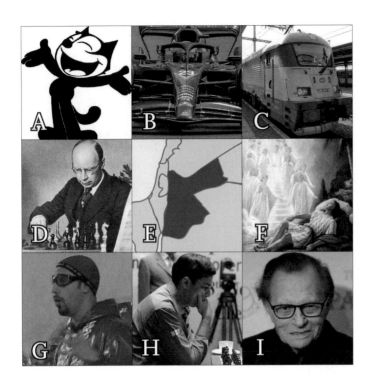

What's the connection? 4

In 1984, Neil Tennant of the Pet Shop Boys had written a song which was supposed to be on their debut album. They needed a female singer for the song but had a hard time finding one.

Someone suggested Dusty Springfield, but their record company didn't agree. Springfield's career had declined sharply, and her last top 40 hit had been in 1970. Tennant, a big fan of Springfield, insisted. The duet was recorded, became a big hit and revived the career of Springfield. It is featured on *Actually*, the first ever album I bought!

1		(4,3,5)
2		(4)
3		(8)
4		(7,7)
5		(4,6)
6		(7)
7		(6,9,6,4) (7,6)
8		(1,4)
9		(4)
10		(3,7,5)

1. What is the name of the debut single of the Pet Shop Boys, that (in re-recorded version) topped the charts in, among others, the US and the UK?

2. What is the basic ingredient of jambalaya?

3. What is the capital of the Italian region Tuscany?

4. Under what name is Farrokh Bulsara better known?

5. The Big Four in tennis are Federer, Nadal, Djokovic and ...?

6. The longest place name is Krung Thep Mahanakhon Amon Rattanakosin Mahinthara Ayuthaya Mahadilok Phop Noppharat Ratchathani Burirom Udomratchaniwet Mahasathan Amon Piman Awatan Sathit Sakkathattiya Witsanukam Prasit. This city is better known under an unofficial name, which one?

7. A World Championship match started with a quiet draw in 18 moves, after which the player with the black pieces supposedly explained, 'We were only testing the equipment.' Six more draws would follow before the first decisive game in Game 8. Which match was this, and who said it?

8. Which two words are repeated 25 times in the song Ain't No Sunshine by Bill Withers?

9. Which band, founded in 1972, got their first-ever Grammy nomination (category Record of the year) in November 2021?

10. Who or what connects the answers to the above questions?

When they were young 5

In the first World Junior Championship, held in 1951 in Birmingham and Coventry, there were 18 participants. Too many for a closed tournament, so the Swiss system was used, but that didn't go so well. Winner Borislav Ivkov had four Whites and seven Blacks, number 16 John Jackson the reverse. Bent Larsen (who finished 4th/6th) suspected favouritism by the organisers and objected several times to the pairings, in some cases with success. Not a ringing endorsement for the Swiss system, and it was only in 1975 that it was used again to decide the World Junior Champion.

In the pictures you see several World Junior contestants. Who are they?

Solution:

Hints on page 120
Solution on page 132

Guess and refute the blunders

I learned chess when I was six, but only joined a chess club at age twelve. Before that I had already studied chess by reading the five chess books in my parents' house, *Prisma Schaakboek* 1 to 5. Reading the books included reading chess games: I was too lazy to play through a game with board and pieces. Fortunately it turned out to be aery good practice for visualisation.

On this page, you can practice both your visualisation and your chess knowledge. The following eleven games are from nine World Champions and two Women's World Champions. In each game, the champion's name and the last move of the game is hidden. Can you guess them?

Game 1 ? vs Voigt Philadelphia 1885
1.e4 c5 2.♘c3 ♘c6 3.♘f3 ♘f6 4.e4 ♘g8 5.d4 cxd4 6.♘xd4 e6 7.♘e4 d5 8.exd6 ♗xd6 9.♗b5 ♕d7 10.c3 ♗b8 11.♘c5 ♕c7 12.0-0 ?

Game 2 Bird vs ? Newcastle on Tyne 1892
1. e4 e5 2. d4 exd4 3. c3 dxc3 4. ♗c4 cxb2 5. ♗xb2 ♕g5 6. ♘f3 ♕xg2 7. ♖g1 ♗b4+ 8. ♔e2 ♕h3 9. ♗xf7+ ♔d8 10. ♗xg7 ♘e7 11. ♘g5 ♕h4 12 ? 1-0

Game 3 Wiersma vs ? Amsterdam 1921
1.d4 d5 2.♘f3 c5 3.c4 e6 4.♘c3 cxd4 5.♘xd4 e5 6.♘f3 d4 7.♘d5 ♘f6 8.♗g5 ♗e6 9.e4 dxe3 10 ? 1-0

Game 4 Kortchnoi vs ? Leningrad 1948
1.e4 c5 2.♘f3 d6 3.d4 cxd4 4.♘xd4 ♘f6 5.♘c3 g6 6.f4 ♗g4 7.♗b5+ ♘bd7 8.♗xd7+ ♕xd7 9.♕d3 e5 10.♘f3 ♗xf3 11.♕xf3 ♕g4 12 ? 1-0

Game 5 ? vs Ree Wijk aan Zee 1971
1.c4 e5 2.♘c3 ♘f6 3.♘f3 ♘c6 4.g3 ♗b4 5.♘d5 ♘xd5 6.cxd5 e4 7.dxc6 exf3 8 ? 1-0

Game 6 Zapata vs ? Biel 1988
1.e4 e5 2.♘f3 ♘f6 3.♘xe5 d6 4.♘f3 ♘xe4 5.♘c3 ♗f5 6 ? 1-0
Bonus question: which grandmaster game had featured the first five moves before and what was the result?

Game 7 Christiansen vs ? Wijk aan Zee 1993
1.d4 ♘f6 2.c4 e6 3.♘f3 b6 4.a3 ♗a6 5.♕c2 ♗b7 6.♘c3 c5 7.e4 cxd4 8.♘xd4 ♘c6 9.♘xc6 ♗xc6 10.♗f4 ♘h5 11.♗e3 ♗d6 12 ? 1-0

Game 8 Willemze vs ? Groningen 1998
1. e4 c5 2.♘f3 d6 3. c3 ♘f6 4. h3 ♗d7 5.♗d3 ♘c6 6.♗c2 g6 7. 0-0 ♗g7 8. d4 cxd4 9.cxd4 ♘b4 10.♗b3 ♘xe4 11 ? 1-0

Game 9 ? vs Lalith Gibraltar 2017
1.g4 d5 2.f3 e5 3.d3 ♕h4+ 4.♔d2 h5 5.h3 ? 0-1
Bonus question: Why did White throw this game?

Game 10 Ding vs ? Chessable Masters 2020
1.c4 e6 2.g3 ♕g5 3.♗g2 ♕xd2+ 4 ? 1-0
Bonus question: Why did Black throw this game?

Game 11 Mamedyarov vs ? Blitz Zagreb 2021
1.d4 d5 2.c4 dxc4 3.e3 e5 4.♘f3 exd4 5.♗xc4 ♘f6 6.♕b3 ♕e7 7 ? 1-0

	Player	Blunder
1		
2		
3		
4		
5		
6		
7		
8		
9		
10		
11		

Bonus Question Game 6	
Bonus Question Game 9	
Bonus Question Game 10	

Celeb64: others

Here you find the celebrities that didn't fit in the other sections. Businessmen, writers, politicians – all of them famous, but not for their chess. Though maybe two of them could have been. One celeb was one of the top players in his country, another celeb was one of the top junior players and still has a FIDE-rating of 2199 (bonus question: who?)

In the hints you can find the nationality and occupation of each celeb.

#														
1	9	5		4						11				
2	8	12			7	4			9					
3				9		1			14					
4	2	5		3			2		5					
5		12							12					
6		5		13		5		5	13		10	13		–	
	14		10											
7		12			1				–					
			1			9								
8			3		3	14						13		
9				12	9					7				
10			5		6			10		10				
11	2					9		6					8	
12		9	1					13	–					
		1												
13	2			7		11								
14	13				3						3		14		
15		10	7	2					14	14				

Solution:

1	2	3	4	5	6	7	8	9	10	11	12	13	14

Hints on page 120
Solution on page 133

Tweets

In the first decennium of this century, blogging was popular. Many people I knew had a blog (and so had I). Everyone could start one, and you could write about anything you liked. Then in 2006, something new was invented – microblogging. It was the same as blogging, except that there was a limit of 140 characters. I didn't understand it: why would you want to limit yourself that way? It gained some popularity, but I thought it would blow over. I was wrong. Few people have an active blog, but about 330 million people have a Twitter account. Including many chess players.

You see ten tweets and ten names of chess players. Who tweeted what?

Person	Tweet
Anish Giri	
Anna Rudolf	
Garry Kasparov	
Hikaru Nakamura	
Judit Polgar	
Magnus Carlsen	
Nigel Short	
Sergey Karjakin	
Susan Polgar	
Teimour Radjabov	

Russian internet joke: "We are now entering day 24 of the special military operation to take Kyiv in two days."

4:40 AM · Mar 19, 2022 · Hootsuite Inc.

19.2K Retweets   721 Quote Tweets   120.2K Likes

1

What really saddens me is that apparently the hacker got me better engagement than my own tweets.

I have to do better. 🤦

10:22 AM · Feb 13, 2022 · Twitter for iPhone

295 Retweets   40 Quote Tweets   12.3K Likes

2

With all respect, Ian, I fully disagree. There's place for any chess event at any level. Pogchamps in particular has opened the door to so many people who wouldn't watch chess otherwise -- and will now possibly tune in to other chess streams too. That's anything but sad.

> Yan Nepomniachtchi @lachesisq · Feb 21, 2021
> With all respect towards @chesscom and amount of work they put into promoting chess, #PogChamps3 as a popcorn stuff is replacing and displacing any real chess content and this is just terrifying. #sad

2:56 AM · Feb 22, 2021 · Twitter for Android

125 Retweets   7 Quote Tweets   2,920 Likes

3

I lost count on how many times in my life I've been called ugly, stupid, fat, useless, no brain, no talent, or far worse, by fans, opponents, and even chess politicians, etc. If I let these words bother me then I would not be here today. A champion has to block everything out!

2:46 AM · Mar 14, 2022 from Johannesburg, South Africa · Twitter for iPad

148 Retweets   13 Quote Tweets

1,737 Likes

4

Call me mr five times

4:47 PM · Dec 12, 2021 · Twitter for iPhone

4,103 Retweets   672 Quote Tweets

92.2K Likes

5

Ok, I asked Ding directly, what is the right way to pronounce? Li-ren or Li-Zhen, i asked him exactly this, pronouncing both, he looked at me and said : I don't see any difference between the two, when you pronounce them. Thus creating more confusion for years to come!

1:22 PM · Jul 5, 2022 · Twitter for iPhone

294 Retweets   36 Quote Tweets   7,409 Likes

6

Of course I congratulate a World Champion, but just a small remark.

Imagine you have to play a World Championship match against Carlsen. Will you accept help from let's say...Hammer or Tari?

10:58 PM · Dec 10, 2021 · Twitter for iPhone

38 Retweets   183 Quote Tweets   850 Likes

7

I recall Boris Spassky once telling me a story of how he once checkmated an opponent. He paused, waiting for the guy to shake hands and sign the scoresheet, but was surprised when his opponent simply made another move. I was reminded of this today seeing @BorisJohnson continue.

4:17 PM · Jul 6, 2022 · Twitter for iPhone

42 Retweets   6 Quote Tweets   523 Likes

8

Sitting cross-legged in Istanbul (2000). At the 1988 Thessaloniki Chess Olympiad (gold medal!) and in chess tournaments afterwards, I always put my legs under me while playing. It helped my concentration, I felt like I was in a cocoon. My look says it all... 😂💪

5:29 PM · May 12, 2021 · TweetDeck

99 Retweets   12 Quote Tweets   1,788 Likes

9

Starting to realize that I am the only person who is going to be able to stop Sauron in the context of chess history.

4:01 AM · Nov 19, 2013 · Twitter Web Client

98 Retweets   17 Quote Tweets   142 Likes

10

Solution on page 134

Women's world champions

One of the biggest German chess talents ever was Jutta Hempel. She was born in 1960. At age 3 she could already replay chess games by memory, at age 6 she scored 9.5 points in a 12 boards simul against senior experts, at age 7 she went 6-0 in a blindfold simul, at age 9 she drew IM Enevoldsen twice. Alas, chess was just a hobby for her, she had other priorities and as a young adult she even stopped playing completely. A German Women's World Champion, it was not to be.

Do you know the Women's World Champions? Probably not all of them, so here are their names. Can you link eleven of them with the following descriptions? Fill in the full names.

Vera Menchik
Lyudmila Rudenko
Elisaveta Bykova
Olga Rubtsova
Nona Gaprindashvili
Maia Chiburdanidze
Xie Jun
Susan Polgar
Zhu Chen
Antoaneta Stefanova
Xu Yuhua
Alexandra Kosteniuk
Hou Yifan
Anna Ushenina
Mariya Muzychuk
Tan Zhongyi
Ju Wenjun.

1. Vice-president of FIDE.

2. A citizen of Qatar.

3. The first woman in the top 50 ratings of the world.

4. Became a professor at age 26.

5. Was handed the mandate for the formation of a government.

6. Filed a lawsuit against Netflix for $5 million.

7. Is listed on IMDB as an actress and a writer.

8. Was vice-champion of her country in breaststroke swimming.

9. Could not defend her world title because of pregnancy.

10. A World Champion, who lost twice against her, was declared the 'president' of her club.

11. Refused to play in the World Championship in which her sister would make the finals.

1		(4th letter)
2		(3rd)
3		(11th)
4		(5th)
5		(8rd)
6		(7th)
7		(11th)
8		(7th)
9		(9th)
10		(4th)
11		(3rd)

Solution:

1	2	3	4	5	6	7	8	9	10	11

Solution on page 134

Photos: movies

After making *Hair*, the Czech American director Miloš Forman agreed to make a movie about the match between Spassky and Fischer, but only if the main characters would play themselves. Spassky agreed; Fischer didn't say no, but his paranoid behaviour annoyed Forman so much that he cancelled the project. Instead, he went on to make a movie about another genius, *Amadeus*, which won eight Oscars.

Alas, there is no chess in that movie, unlike the twelve movies in the pictures. Do you know the titles? When it is a sequel, the main title is enough.

1	13			10				4		—				
	1			9	15									
2		10	7			15				10				
3	13	14		7		17			13		8			15
4		15				12								
5		10		18			6							
6	8		9				3	2						
7		6	8						11		5			
8		2		13		11	16							
9					10	7				18	—			
	3				7	18								
10		14			9		15			16				12
11	5													
12		4												

Solution:

1	2	3	4	5	6	7	8	9	10

11	12	13	14	15	16	17	18

What's in a name? 3

Sometimes Wikipedia adds (chess player) to a grandmaster's name, to distinguish from other people with the same name. Take for example Michael Rohde: he is not only an American grandmaster born in 1959, but also a Danish football player (1894-1979) and a German botanist (1782-1812). But that's nothing compared to grandmaster No. 10 in the list below. There are fifteen other people with the same name on Wikipedia!

1. 5...a6

2. USSR champion 1985 – changed federations thrice

3. Learned chess at age 12 – electrical engineer

4. Unbeaten streak records in 1973 and 1974

5. U cannot be serious – Grob

6. chess.com director of content – FunMasterMike

7. Ukrainian Slovenian

8. Learn from the Legends – The English Opening

9. Variations named after in Ruy Lopez and Queen's Gambit

10. Semi-finalist in 1999 and 2000 FIDE World Championships

11. Youngest Argentine champion – three-year FIDE ban in 1987

12. Moscow-born Polish – King's Indian variation

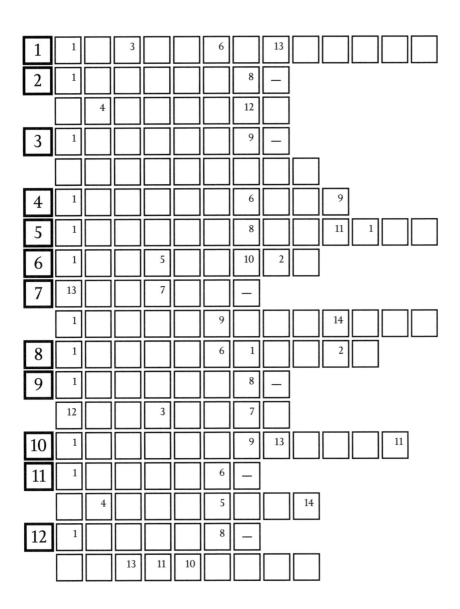

Solution:

1	2	3	4	5	6	7	8	9	10	11	12	13	14

Solution on page 135

Celeb64: sports

Sometimes people pose behind a chessboard for a picture. They don't play chess, but they hope it makes them looks smarter! Such a poseur can be seen in picture 3. The bottom right square being black is one thing, but playing without a king, really? He is an exception though: most of the other athletes are real chess players!

#														
1	3		5	5			6				13	6	
2	8			2	2		3	4				4	
3				13	14				11				
4	5				8								
5		9	14				9			1			
6				10		12			12				
7	1				8		2						
8	3		6				10		6				
9			4					5	11				
10		13		11	—								
			3						13	14			
11		4		7		6		2			6		
12	3	13			1								
13		6				3	—						
	6		8				6			6			
14		2	11				—						
			2	11	1								
15		10		6				6			13		12	10

106

Solution:

1	2	3	4	5	6	7	8	9	10	11	12	13	14

Solution on page 135

Ranking the Stars: Megabase games

How many games should someone play per year? Botvinnik once suggested to play about sixty serious games per year (he didn't like fast formats: a famous quote is 'Yes. I have played a blitz game once. It was on a train, in 1929.') According to Megabase, Botvinnik himself played 873 games between his 18th and 50th birthday, about 27 per year. There will be some games/tournaments missing, but still.

For Firouzja, Megabase has 544 games from 2021 alone! Though most of them are not exactly what Botvinnik would call 'serious games'. He is not yet in the top ten of players with the most games, but very likely will be in the future.

In the current top ten are... well, that's up to you to guess. To help you, the nationality and amount of games for each player is given. You only need to give their surnames.

1: USA, 6166 games

2: Switzerland, 5171 games

3: Spain, 4844 games

4: Hungary, 4748 games

5: Ukraine, 4683 games

6: Russia, 4594 games

7: Norway, 4535 games

8: The Netherlands, 4416 games

9: USA, 4427 games

10: USA, 4352 games

1		5		5			6		
2			6	1	4				3
3		8	9			10			
4		5	6	5					
5	9	10			7	8			
6			3		4	8			
7	7					11			
8		5		2	11				
9		5							
10	5	6			3	5			

Solution:

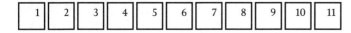

1	2	3	4	5	6	7	8	9	10	11

Solution on page 135

Photo Connection: cities

The largest city of the world according to Wikipedia is Tokyo. The UN 2018 population estimates 37,468,000 people living there. Very few of them play chess, Japan has 312 rated chess players. There are quite a few chess clubs in Tokyo, but most of them meet only once or twice a month. The Japanese have their own chess variant, Shogi, which is much more popular. To play chess, it's better to live in one of the cities 1 to 9. Can you link them with the pictures A-I and R-Z?

	A-I	R-Z		A-I	R-Z		A-I	R-Z
1			4			7		
2			5			8		
3			6			9		

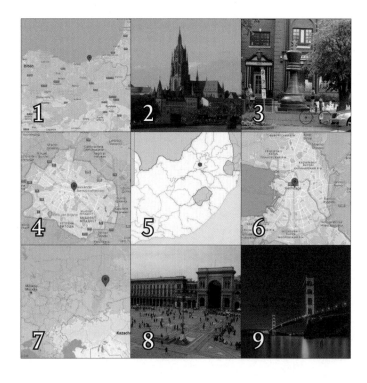

What's the connection? 5

Top cyclists very often get nicknames with some kind of animal in them.
Here are a few examples: Johan Museeuw: the Lion of Flanders. Bernard
Hinault: le Blaireau (badger). Vincenzo Nibali: the Shark of Messina.
Robert Gesink: the Condor of Varsseveld. Tom Dumoulin: the Butterfly of
Maastricht. This is not the case with jazz musicians, they get nicknames
like Duke, Doc, Buddy or Sonny. Though one of the most famous did get
an animal nickname. Do you know it?

1		(4)
2		(9,4)
3		(6,7)
4		(3,8,7)
5		(7,6)
6		(3,3,3,2)
7		(6,6)
8		(7,8)
9		(3,7,11)
10		(3,5)

1. What is the four-letter nickname of jazz saxophonist Charlie Parker?

2. Which worldwide bestseller by Haruki Murakami has a title based on a song of the Beatles?

3. Which grandmaster defeated Galliamova (2547) at age 80 in the Klompendans tournament in Amsterdam?

4. Which island country has their own cryptocurrency SOV (sovereign) as legal tender since 2018, next to the dollar?

5. Who has played the most World Championship matches?

6. The debut single by the English new wave band Bow Wow Wow was the world's first ever cassette single. Both the title and the lyrics refer to cassettes. What is the title?

7. Wikipedia says, 'Since its release, *White Christmas* has been covered by many artists, the version sung by Bing Crosby being the world's best-selling single (in terms of sales of physical media) with estimated sales in excess of 50 million copies worldwide. When the figures for other versions of the song are added to Crosby's, sales of the song exceed 100 million.' But who wrote it?

8. Who is widely regarded as the founder of the Russian School of Chess?

9. Amongst whose weaponry are such diverse elements as: fear, surprise, ruthless efficiency, an almost fanatical devotion to the Pope, and nice red uniforms?

10. Who or what connects the answers to the above questions?

Hints on page 120
Solution on page 136

When they were young 6

Organising the World Youth Championships is a challenge. More and more categories were added through the years, and therefore more players and accompanying adults needed accommodation. In 2015, the wise decision was made to split the tournament in World Cadets Chess Championships (U8, U10, U12) and the World Youth Chess Championships (U14, U16, U18).

Do you recognize four world youth champions and eight of their rivals in the pictures?

#													
1	16		4				10	—					
	10		5				3	2					
2				11					1	7	11		
3		13	13					18				13	
4	15				15				18	—			
	14			6	14								
5	11		17				11				10		16
6	8				4	19		3					
7	5			6	5			11			18	7	
8	17			19				9			17		3	2
9	11				7			4					
10			13			6			18	—			
	2	13				18	12	18					
11	1		11		1			11	14	—			
	8	14											
12	15				5	17		—					
	19		17		17	16							

114

Hints on page 120
Solution on page 135

Solution:

1	2	3	4	5	6	7	8

9	10	11	12	13	14	15	16	17	18	19

Leftovers

Congratulations for making it to the end of the book! As a dessert I have some leftover non-related questions. No hints, no letters given by an acrostic, you either know the answer or must guess. Good luck!

1. Adolf Anderssen played some famous games. Who were his opponents in The Immortal Game and The Evergreen Game?

2. Steinitz, Lasker, Capablanca and Alekhine all became World Champions. But what important chess title didn't they get (but I did)?

3. In 1918, the later grandmaster Ossip Bernstein was about to be shot by a firing squad. How did he (by his own account) save his life?

4. Sir George Thomas was a very capable chess player, twice British champion. However, in another sport he was one of the best of the world and the long-time president of the international federation. They named the Thomas Cup after him. Which sport is that?

5. In 1946, the Dutch chess club Schaakgezelschap Staunton organised the famous Groningen Chess Tournament, won by Botwinnik. It almost meant bankruptcy for the club, but not because of the organisation costs. What was the reason for the big financial setback?

6. The first Lithuanian head of state after their independence from the Soviet Union was a grand master. Grand Master Grand Cross with Collar of the Order of Vytautas the Great, to be exact. But maybe, if his life had turned out differently, he could have become a chess grandmaster: in 1952 he placed third in the Lithuanian championship. What is his name?

7. In 1975, Fischer refused to defend his title, the reason being that not all his match conditions were accepted. Actually, most of them were, but there was one rule that was rejected by an extraordinary FIDE Congress with 32 votes for and 35 votes against. What rule was that?

8. Who was considered the strongest Asian player during the 1960s and 1970s?

9. Kortchnoi-Karpov, Candidates 1974 (21). Black had just taken a bishop on d5. Why did White contact the arbiter here?

10. Which chess player has a small role (15 seconds) in the 1981 movie Ragtime by Miloš Forman?

11. In the 2005 Hoogeveen Chess Tournament, the brilliancy prize was awarded to the following game. Black is a celebrity in his own land. Why?
Peter Wells (2513)-Yoshiharu Habu (2341) 1.d4 d5 2.c4 c6 3.♘f3 ♘f6 4.♘c3 e6 5.e3 ♘bd7 6.♗d3 dxc4 7.♗xc4 b5 8.♗e2 b4 9.♘a4 ♗d6 10.e4 ♘xe4 11.♕c2 f5 12.♘g5 ♘xg5 13.♕xc6 ♘e4 14.♕xa8 O-O 15.♕c6 ♘df6 16.f3 ♗d7 17.♕a6 ♗xa4 18.♕xa4 ♗xh2 19. ♖xh2 ♕xd4 20.fxe4 ♘xe4 21.♖h1 ♕f2+ 22.♔d1 ♖d8+ 23.♔c2 ♕xe2+ 24.♔b1 ♘c3+ 25.bxc3 bxc3 26.♗a3 ♖b8+ 27.♕b3 ♕d3+ 28. ♔c1 ♕d2+ 0-1

12. Another Japanese chess player is WIM Miyoko Watai, rated 2032. What is she best known for in the chess world?

13. What is remarkable about amateur group 5K of the 2015 Tata Steel tournament?

1	Georgiev, Alexander	1750S	3.0	3.00	2078
2	Geer, Dirk van de	1713	1.5	0.75	1755
2	Visser, Ingmar	1757	1.5	0.75	1741
4	Doggenaar, Hans van	1760	0.0	0.00	1411

14. What is the name of the opening that consists of the moves 1.e4 e5 2.♔e2 ♔e7 ?

15. Why did Daniil Dubov withdraw from the Tata Steel Tournament 2022 and in which round?

16. Which country has the most grandmasters per capita?

17. What is happening in the next pictures?

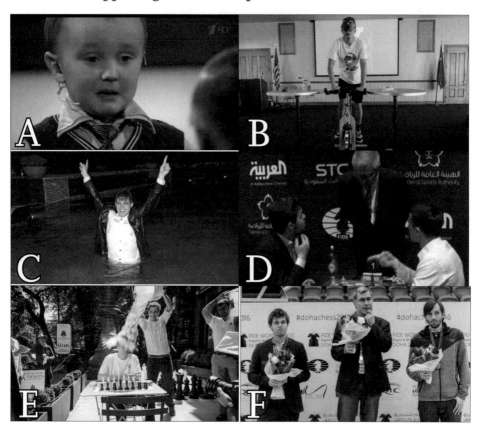

Solution on page 135

Hints

Guess the moves
1. Amsterdam 1889
2. Zurich 1953
3. Sochi 1958
4. Belgrade 1970 (USSR vs. the world)
5. Nice 1974
6. Tilburg 1989
7. Tilburg 1991
8. Sveti Stefan 1992
9. Wijk aan Zee 1995
10. Wijk aan Zee 2013
11. Jerusalem 2015
12. New York 2016

When they were young 1
Eight of the twelve players have been World Champions. 4, 5 and 8 have played for the world title. The odd one out is 7 whose best world ranking was #11 in 1978 (and who is still active; he played 80 rated games in 2022!)
The solution consists of two abilities that help one to make it to the top.

Chess players and their eyes
The players are from China, France, Georgia, India, Russia (2x), Sweden, Ukraine, United Kingdom, United States.

What's the connection? 1
The answer to question 10 is a well-known grandmaster.

Anagrams
Start with the shortest anagrams. Also, you might find the answer on 11 on the front cover of the book.

When they were young 2
The current (chess) nationalities of the girls: 1. Indian 2. Lithuanian 3. Romanian 4. Russian 5. Georgian 6. Ukrainian 7. American 8. Russian 9. German 10. Russian 11. Indian 12. Chinese
The solution is one of the strongest girl players of the world.

What's the connection? 2
The answer to question 10 is a movie.

When they were young 3
The years of birth of the players:
1. 1987 2. 1991 3. 1992 4. 2004 5. 1993 6. 1986 7. 1988 8. 1969 9. 1993 10. 2003 11. 1992 12. 2006
The solution is a legendary Asian player from the past.

Photo Connection: pop music
Famous songs 1 to 9:
1. (They Long to Be) Close to You
2. Wonderful Tonight
3. Despacito
4. To All the Girls I've Loved Before
5. Uptown Girl
6. Only Love
7. The Gambler
8. Show Me Love
9. Sign of the Times

What's the connection? 3
Answers 1 to 8 can be related to famous players. In what tournament in the country of 9 did those players meet?

Logos

Of the answers, three are mostly known as an abbreviation, thirteen are normally written in full. Only three of those don't have the word chess in them. Three answers are organisations; one is cultural, one a tournament, one a chess club, seven offer premium/pro membership. Two answers have a country in their name, one a city, one includes numbers.

When they were young 4

The current (chess) nationalities of the boys: 1. French 2. Romanian 3. Russian 4. Polish 5. Norwegian 6. Dutch 7. Russian 8. American 9. American 10. Dutch 11. Norwegian 12. British

What's the connection? 4

There is a musical connection between the answers.

When they were young 5

The current (chess) nationalities of the boys: 1. Dutch 2. Dutch 3. German 4. American 5. Israeli 6. Canadian 7. British 8. German 9. American 10. Dutch 11. American 12. British

Celeb64: others

1. Russian writer
2. German-American billionaire entrepreneur
3. American business magnate
4. Israeli politician
5. German playwright
6. Irish playwright
7. American polymath
8. British humanitarian
9. Cuban politician
10. Argentine icon

11. French artist
12. Russian-American writer
13. American photographer
14. British business magnate
15. Estonian model

Photos: movies

The alphabetical order (excluding 'The') is 1 to 10, 2 to 11, 3 to 12.

Photo Connection: cities

The cities are in alphabetical order 2 5 8 3 6 9 1 4 7.
The chess players are in alphabetical order (first name) V Y Z W T S R U X.

What's the connection? 5

You might have had the connection on the board.

When they were young 6

The current (chess) nationalities of the boys: 1. Azerbaijani 2. British 3. Georgian 4. American 5. French 6. British 7. Australian 8. Bulgarian 9. Dutch 10. Spanish 11. Russian 12. Azerbaijani

Solutions

Guess the moves

1. **Lasker-Bauer**, Amsterdam 1889. The double bishop sacrifice on h7 and g7 is often called the Lasker-Bauer combination after this game: **15.♗xh7+! ♔xh7 16.♕xh5+ ♔g8 17.♗xg7! ♔xg7 18.♕g4+ ♔h7 19.♖f3 e5 20.♖h3+ ♕h6 21.♖xh6+ ♔xh6** Black has rook and two bishops for queen and two pawns, but both bishops are undefended. So: **22.♕d7!** This is the point of the combination. White wins one of the bishops and the rest is easy. **22...♗f6 23.♕xb7 ♔g7 24.♖f1 ♖ab8 25.♕d7 ♖fd8 26.♕g4+ ♔f8 27.fxe5 ♗g7 28. e6 ♖b7 29.♕g6 f6 30.♖xf6+ ♗xf6 31.♕xf6+ ♔e8 32.♕h8+ ♔e7 33.♕g7+ ♔xe6 34.♕xb7 ♖d6 35.♕xa6 d4 36.exd4 cxd4 37. h4 d3 38.♕xd3 1-0**

2. **Averbakh-Kotov**, Zurich 1953. The brilliancy of the following magnet combination is that there isn't a forced mate, but there is no defence for White either. White can avoid mate (in the short run), but only with heavy material costs: **30...♕xh3+!! 31.♔xh3 ♖h6+ 32.♔g4 ♘f6+ 33.♔f5 ♘d7 34.♖g5 ♖f8+ 35. ♔g4 ♘f6+ 36.♔f5 ♘g8+ 37.♔g4 ♘f6+ 38.♔f5 ♘xd5+ 39.♔g4 ♘f6+ 40.♔f5 ♘g8+ 41.♔g4 ♘f6+ 42.♔f5 ♘g8+ 43.♔g4 ♗xg5 44.♔xg5 ♖f7 45.♗h4 ♖g6+ 46.♔h5 ♖fg7 47.♗g5 ♖xg5+ 48.♔h4 ♘f6 49.♘g3 ♖xg3 50.♕xd6 ♖3g6 51.♕b8+ ♖g8 0-1**

3. **Polugaevsky-Nezhmetdinov**, Sochi 1958. Again the white king is lured into the open field, but this time he is mated quickly: **24...♖xf4!!**
25.♖xh2 ♖f3+ 26.♔d4 ♗g7 27. a4 c5+ 28.dxc6 bxc6 29.♗d3 ♘exd3+ 30.♔c4 d5+ 31.exd5 cxd5+ 32.♔b5 ♖b8+ 33.♔a5 ♘c6+ 0-1

4. **Lasker-Spassky**, Belgrade 1970. **14...♖h1!?** Often called a brilliant move, and it probably is, but it might also be called gallery play. It's actually only the fourth choice of SF 15! 14...♗xe3, 14...♕h4 and 14...g2 are also winning. **15.♖xh1 g2 16. ♖f1 ♕h4+ 17.♔d1 gxf1♕+ 0-1**

5. **Karpov-Unzicker**, Nice 1974. **24.♗a7!** A strong positional move. White, who has more space, prevents pieces being exchanged. Next he will double on the a-file and then start an attack on the king's side: **24...♘e8 25.♗c2 ♘c7 26.♖ea1 ♕e7 27.♗b1 ♗e8 28.♘e2 ♘d8 29.♘h2 ♗g7 30. f4 f6 31. f5 g5 32.♗c2 ♗f7 33.♘g3 ♘b7 34.♗d1 h6 35.♗h5 ♕e8 36.♕d1 ♘d8 37.♖a3 ♔f8 38.♖1a2 ♔g8 39.♘g4 ♔f8 40. ♘e3 ♔g8 41.♗xf7+ ♘xf7 42.♕h5 ♘d8 43.♕g6 ♔f8 44.♘h5 1-0**

6. **Piket-Kasparov**, Tilburg 1989. In an exemplary King's Indian game, Kasparov applied the finishing touch by bringing his queen into play: **25...a6! 26.♕d3 ♕a7 27. b5 axb5 28.♗xb5 ♘h1 0-1**

7. **Short-Timman**, Tilburg 1991. The king walk of king walks: **32.♔g3!** and Black has no good defence against the white king going to h6. **32...♖ce8 33.♔f4 ♗c8 34.♔g5! 1-0**

8. **Fischer-Spassky**, Sveti Stefan 1992. In the controversial revenge match, Fischer showed that he was still a strong player: **19.♘bxc5! ♗c8 20.♘xa6 fxe5 21.♘b4 1-0**

121

9. **Cifuentes-Zvjaginsev**, Wijk aan Zee 1995. This game is known as The pearl of Wijk aan Zee. **24...♘xf2! 25.♔xf2 ♖xe3! 26.♗xe3 ♘g4+ 27.♔f3 ♘xh2+ 28.♔f2 ♘g4+ 29.♔f3 ♕e6! 30.♗f4 ♖e8 31.♕c4 ♕e3+!** The quickest (though not only) winning move: a forced mate in six. **32.♗xe3 ♖xe3+ 33.♔xg4 ♗c8+ 34.♔g5 h6+! 35.♔xh6 ♖e5 0-1**

10. **Aronian-Anand**, Wijk aan Zee 2013. Anand called this game one of the best of his life. There was one move he was especially proud of: **16...♘de5!** There is no defence for White after this move. **17.♗xg4 ♗xd4+ 18.♔h1 ♘xg4 19.♘xf8 f5! 20.♘g6 ♕f6 21.h3 ♕xg6 22.♕e2 ♕h5 23.♕d3 ♗e3 0-1**

11. **Khismatullin-Eljanov**, Jerusalem 2015. **44.♔g1!!** A great move, hanging a rook with check. There is still a defence for Black, but few people would have found it. **44...♕xd1+?** After 44...♖d5! 45.♔h2 ♔f6!. There is no forced win for White, though he still has some pressure after 46.e4. After the game move Black is lost. **45.♔h2 ♖xc6 46. ♕e7+ ♔h6 47.♕f8+ ♔g5 48.♕xf7! ♖f6 49. f4+ ♔h6 50.♕xf6 ♕e2 51. ♕f8+ ♔h5 52.♕g7 h6 53.♕e5+ ♔h4 54.♕f6+ ♔h5 55. f5 gxf5 56. ♕xf5+ ♔h4 57.♕g6 1-0**

12. **Carlsen-Karjakin**, New York 2016. This was the fourth and last rapid game of the tiebreak of the 2016 World Championship match. Karjakin needed a win to tie, but it was Carlsen who finished the match with a very nice move: **50.♕h6+! 1-0** However Black takes, it is mate next move.

When they were young 1
1. Boris Spassky
2. Anatoly Karpov
3. Garry Kasparov
4. Viktor Kortchnoi
5. Samuel Reshevsky
6. Alexander Alekhine
7. Oleg Romanishin
8. David Bronstein
9. José Raúl Capablanca
10. Bobby Fischer
11. Mikhail Tal
12. Max Euwe
Solution: Savvy and able

Fair & Square 1: grandmasters
Hein Donner 7
Ivan Sokolov 9
Magnus Carlsen 1
Peter Leko 6
Peter Svidler 4
Sergei Tiviakov 8
Vladimir Kramnik 5
Walter Browne 2
Wilhelm Steinitz 3

Chess players and their eyes
1. Garry Kasparov
2. Wei Yi
3. Nigel Short
4. Humpy Koneru
5. Ulf Andersson
6. Joel Lautier
7. Vasyl Ivanchuk
8. Wesley So
9. Baadur Jobava
10. Mikhail Tal
11. Ivan Sokolov
12. Kateryna Lagno
13. Hans Niemann
14. Genna Sosonko
Solution: Visualisations

What's the connection? 1

1. Stuart Little
2. Garry Kasparov
3. Athens (Greece)
4. The Prodigy
5. 1965
6. English
7. XTC
8. Steel King (or fighting king, king walk, king march according to Wikipedia). I prefer the Dutch term though: 'Winnende wandelkoning', i.e. winning walking king.
9. Vice
10. Nigel Short. Born in 1965, the English grandmaster was a prodigy in his youth. He played Kasparov for the PCA world title. From 2018 to 2022 he was Vice-President of FIDE. He lives in Athens. He famously beat Timman in 1991 with a steel king. The band XTC is best known by their song Making plans for Nigel. Little is another word for short.

Photo Connection: countries

1 I T: Danish Gambit – Danish Pastry – Bent Larsen
2 G U: Icelandic Gambit – Icelandic Horse – Helgi Ólafsson
3 B V: English Defence – Johnny English – John Nunn
4 D R: Polish Defence – Nail Polish – Jan-Krzysztof Duda
5 E Y: Armenian Variation (French Defence) – the word French in Armenian – Charles Aznavour (French-Armenian singer)
6 C W: Hungarian Defence – Arpad Elo (Hungarian born) – Peter Leko
7 F X: Austrian Attack (Pirc Defence) – Austrian Airlines – Markus Ragger
8 H Z: Dutch Defense – Refresh (F5-button) – Jeroen Piket

9 A S: Czech Defense (or Pribyl System) – Václav Havel – David Navara

Anagrams

1. Pia Cramling
2. Michael Adams
3. Lucas van Foreest
4. Vladimir Fedoseev
5. Nona Gaprindashvili
6. Alexandra Kosteniuk
7. Sergei Tiviakov
8. Tigran Petrosian
9. Jeroen Piket
10. Nigel Short
11. Dimitri Reinderman
12. Boris Gelfand
13. Wesley So
14. Matthew Sadler
15. Daniil Dubov
Solution: Transposing

Guess the blunders

1. In **Petrosian**-Bronstein, Amsterdam 1956, White didn't notice that his queen was attacked: **36.♘g5?? ♘xd6 0-1**
2. **Kramnik** thought he was winning against Deep Fritz with **34...♛e3??** but alas: **35.♛h7#** Instead, 34...♚g8 would have drawn.
3. In the 1892 World Championship Match between **Chigorin** and Steinitz, White spoiled a winning position in Game 23 by missing mate in two: **32.♗b4?? ♖xh2 0-1**
4. Another World Championship match: **Nepomniachtchi**-Carlsen, Game 9. The position is balanced, but not after **37.c5?? c6** and the bishop on b7 is trapped.
5. The World Champion also blunders pieces. In **Carlsen**-Jones, Wijk aan Zee 2018, after **17.g4?? f4** there were two white pieces

hanging. White does get some vague compensation though and even won the game!

6. Lasker-**Euwe**, Nottingham 1936. Black would be a bit better after 23...♘b6. Instead, after **23...♗a5?? 24.b4! ♗xb4 25.♘c2** Euwe lost a piece and later the game against the 67-year-old veteran.

7. In **Karpov**-Kasparov, World Championship Match 1987, Game 11, 35.♗b4 would have given White a winning position. The tables were turned after **35.♖c6?? ♘a5!** and Black won. The result of the match was 12-12.

8. You may have read about this position in Hein Donner's The King. In the Capablanca Memorial (Havana 1965), **Ivkov** was playing the tournament of his life. Having beaten Smyslov and Fischer, he was leading with two rounds to go. Smyslov and Geller shared second place, a point behind, and drew their mutual game in the penultimate game. Meanwhile Ivkov had a totally winning position against tail-ender Garcia, two pawns and an exchange up. Donner was watching and thought 'This cannot go wrong for Black' but then 'Oh no, it can, he shouldn't push his d-pawn!' And right at that moment there followed **36... d3??? 37.♗c3 1-0**. Ivkov also lost in the last round and finished shared second with Geller and Fischer, half a point behind Smyslov.

9. In the 2015 Fide World Cup final, Karjakin and **Svidler** were tied 4-4. In the first 5-minute blitz game, Svidler got a winning position. He had just played 41...♕d7-b7+ and forgot that after 42.♔h2 his rook wasn't defended anymore: **42...♔g8? 43.♕xb8+ 1-0** If you like tragedies, you can view this game on YouTube.

10. **Kortchnoi**-Karpov, World Championship Match 1978, Game 17. White had missed a win a few moves before, but 39.g3 or 39.g4 still draws. However, isn't **39.♖a1** winning? It would be, if not for **39...♘f3+! 0-1** with a forced mate after 40.gxf3 ♖g6+ 41.♔h1 ♘f2 mate. The result was 16.5-15.5 for Karpov.

11. Quoting Wikipedia: '**Shirazi**'s rating rose rapidly, and he became one of the highest rated players in the United States Chess Federation. However, when invited to play in the 1984 U.S. Chess Championship, Shirazi managed only one draw from 17 games, finishing last. In that championship, Shirazi also achieved the dubious distinction of losing the shortest decisive game in the history of the U.S. Championship: his game as White against John Peters, which went 1.e4 c5 2.b4 cxb4 3.a3 d5 4.exd5 ♕xd5 **5.axb4?? ♕e5+ 0-1.**'

12. **Firouzja**-Carlsen, Stavanger 2020. White had done a good job defending an endgame a pawn down. The pawn endgame is an elementary draw after 69.♔d2, but he must have had a blackout: **69.♔c3?? ♔c5 0-1**

Celeb64: movies

1. Woody Allen
2. Leonard Nimoy
3. Rosemary Clooney
4. Ava Gardner
5. Danny DeVito
6. Marlene Dietrich
7. Shirley Temple

8. Faye Dunaway
9. James Dean
10. Peter Falk
11. Cary Grant
12. Catherine Deneuve
13. Steve McQueen
14. Bobby Darin
15. Stanley Kubrick
Solution: Humphrey Bogart

Ranking the stars: 2000s Olympiads
1 China
2 Russia
3 Ukraine
4 Armenia
5 USA
6 Georgia
7 Uzbekistan
8 Hungary
9 Israel
10 Poland
11 Germany
12 India
Solution: Chennai

What's in a name? 1
1. Alexander Alekhine
2. Alexander Beliavsky
3. Alexander Kotov
4. Alexandra Kosteniuk
5. Alex Yermolinsky
6. Alexander Grischuk
7. Hugh Alexander
8. Alexander Nikitin
9. Alexander Morozevich
10. Alexandr Fier
11. Alexander Khalifman
12. Nana Alexandria
Solution: Alexander Ivanov

When they were young 2
1. Humpy Koneru
2. Viktorija Čmilytė
3. Alina l'Ami

4. Tatiana Kosintseva
5. Nana Dzagnidze
6. Muzychuk (Anna and Mariya)
7. Irina Krush
8. Valentina Gunina
9. Elisabeth Paehtz
10. Kateryna Lagno
11. Dronavalli Harika
12. Hou Yifan
Solution: Govhar Beydullayeva
(the 2022 U20 girls world champion)

Timeline of chess history
1. 1851
2. 1946
3. 1834
4. 1769
5. 1924
6. 1950
7. 1726
8. 1927
9. 1883
10. 1858
11. 1886
12. 1795

Wikipedia
1. Liren Ding
2. Raymond Keene
3. Leonid Stein
4. Eugenio Torre
5. Vladimir Kramnik
6. Henrique Mecking
7. Anna Cramling
8. Anna Muzychuk
9. Teimour Radjabov
10. Amon Simutowe
11. Lev Polugaevsky
12. Zurab Azmaiparashvili
Solution: Peak Rating

Chess players with a beard and/or a moustache
1. Stuart Conquest
2. Yasser Seirawan

3. Ian Rogers
4. Magnus Carlsen
5. Parham Maghsoodloo
6. Yan Nepomniachtchi
7. Hikaru Nakamura
8. Gukesh D
9. Vlastimil Hort
10. Hein Donner
11. Maxime Vachier-Lagrave
12. Bessel Kok
13. Vladimir Epishin
14. Artur Yusupov
15. Emanuel Lasker
16. Sam Shankland

Solution: Trimming the beard

What's the connection? 2
1. Boris Becker
2. Fischer-Z
3. Pawn shop
4. Reykjavik
5. Sacrifice
6. Tobey Maguire
7. *Paranoid*
8. Bobby
9. 1972
10. *Pawn Sacrifice*. This movie is about the 1972 match between Boris Spassky and Bobby Fischer (played by Tobey Maguire) in Reykjavik. An important theme is the paranoia of Fischer.

Photo Connection: political leaders
1 D U: Boris Johnson (UK) – Boris Karloff (as Frankenstein) – Boris Gulko
2 C S: Alexander Lukashenko (Belarus) – Alexandria (second biggest city of Egypt) – Aleksander Delchev
3 B Z: Vladimir Putin (Russia) – Vladimir Horowitz – Vladimir Tukmakov

4 E X: George Weah (Liberia) – St. George Defence – Georg Meier
5 H W: Emmanuel Macron (France) – *Emmanuelle* (the movie) – Emanuel Lasker
6 F Y: Justin Trudeau (Canada) – Justine Henin – Justin Tan
7 G T: Joseph Biden (USA) – Saint Joseph – Joseph Gallagher
8 A R: Viktor Orbán (Hungary) – *Les Misérables* (by Victor Hugo) – Viktorija Čmilytė-Nielsen
9 I V: Xi Jinping (China) – Xi (Greek letter) – Xie Jun

World Champions
1. Tal (World Champion for 1 year and 5 days)
2. Euwe
3. Botvinnik (Born in Kuokkala in 1911 when Finland was part of the Russian Empire)
4. Spassky
5. Alekhine
6. Kasparov ('Whether you spell Garry with a G or an H in Russian, you still pronounce it with a strong G. I was named after President Truman – Harry – whom my father admired for taking a strong stand against communism. It was a rare name in Russia, until Harry Potter came along.')
7. Karpov (in a 2021 interview on chess24.com, he claimed, 'I overtook him – I have 185 wins. That's from the moment I became a Master of Sport, not counting children's and junior tournaments.')
8. Capablanca (in Havana, 1921)
9. Smyslov (1948-1984)
10. Fischer (Paul Felix Nemenyi was his biological father)

11. Lasker (in 1935 he moved to the USSR and received Soviet citizenship. In 1937 he moved to the USA)
12. Steinitz (1836-1900)
13. Petrosian
Solution: Two-year cycles

Chess books
1. *1.d4 Volume One* (Boris Avrukh)
2. *The Woodpecker Method* (Axel Smith & Hans Tikkanen)
3. *My Great Predecessors* (Garry Kasparov)
4. *Game Changer* (Matthew Sadler & Natasha Regan)
5. *Tal-Botwinnik* (1960; Mikhail Tal)
6. *Dvoretsky's Endgame Manual* (Mark Dvoretsky)
7. *Silman's Complete Endgame Course* (Jeremy Silman)
8. *Chess for Zebras* (Jonathan Rowson)
9. *Curacao 1962* (Jan Timman)
10. *100 Endgames You Must Know* (Jesus de la Villa)
11. *Keep It Simple 1.e4* (Christof Sielecki)
12. *Secrets of Opening Surprises* (Editor Jeroen Bosch)
Solution: Opening Books

Fair & Square 2: singers, actors and writers
Anne Brontë 1
Anya Taylor-Joy 8
Björk 9
Charles Bukowski 6
Charli XCX 5
Jerry Seinfeld 7
Stephen Fry 2
Steve Carell 4
Woody Allen 3

Celeb64: movies and TV
1. Antonio Banderas
2. Arnold Schwarzenegger
3. David Letterman
4. Forest Whitaker
5. Howard Stern
6. Hugh Laurie
7. Jason Statham
8. Keanu Reeves
9. Kevin Spacey
10. Kim Kardashian
11. Liam Neeson
12. Rami Malek
13. Robin Williams
14. Stephen Fry
15. Will Smith
Solution: Mating with the stars

Nicknames
1. Alexander Alekhine (he was known to drink a lot of alcohol)
2. Manuel Bosboom (the book about him is called *Chess Buccaneer*)
3. Vasyl Ivanchuk
4. Magnus Carlsen (after he stopped drinking, he became DrNyksterstein: nykter is Norwegian for sober)
5. Simon Williams
6. Milan Matulović (Wikipedia says: 'Perhaps Matulović's most notorious transgression was against István Bilek at the Sousse Interzonal in 1967. He played a losing move but then took it back after saying "j'adoube" ("I adjust" – spoken before adjusting pieces on their square, see touch-move rule). His opponent complained to the arbiter, but the move was allowed to stand. This incident earned Matulović the nickname "J'adoubovic". This reportedly happened several times, including in a game against Bobby Fischer.' He has done worse though: he was convicted of vehicular

manslaughter and served nine months in prison for a car accident in which a woman was killed)
7. Sergey Karjakin
8. Andrew Tang
9. Anish Giri (A #girijoke, he is called The Artist because he likes to draw)
10. Garry Kasparov
11. John Nunn
12. Bent Larsen
13. José Raúl Capablanca
14. Mikhail Botvinnik
15. Evgeny Tomashevsky (partly for being a mostly positional player, partly for wearing glasses and being well-educated, Tomashevsky earned himself the nickname 'Professor' among the chess players)
16. Vishy Anand
17. Semyon Furman (coach of Karpov and an opening specialist)
Solution: Kournikova of chess (a nickname that has been given to both Alexandra Kosteniuk and Arianne Caoili)

When they were young 3
1. Hikaru Nakamura
2. Le Quang Liem
3. Ding Liren
4. Nodirbek Abdusattorov
5. Parimarjan Negi
6. Tania Sachdev
7. Timur Gareyev
8. Vishy Anand
9. Wesley So
10. Alireza Firouzja
11. Baskaran Adhiban
12. Gukesh D
Solution: Mir Sultan Khan (the South Asian chess player who was world class in the early 1930's)

Players who represented at least three federations
1 Levon Aronian (Armenia, Germany, USA)
2 Roberto Cifuentes (Chile, Netherlands, Spain)
3 Robert Fontaine (France, Monaco, Switzerland)
4 Arkadij Naiditsch (Latvia, Germany, Azerbaijan)
5 Alexander Ipatov (Ukraine, Spain, Turkey)
6 Mikhail Gurevich (USSR, Belgium, Turkey)
7 Roman Dzindzichashvili (USSR, Israel, USA)
8 Sergei Movsesian (USSR, Georgia, Czech Republic, Slovakia, Armenia)
9 Igors Rausis (USSR, Latvia, Bangladesh, Czech Republic; former grandmaster actually)
10 Igor Glek (USSR, Russia, Germany, Belgium)
11 Vadim Milov (USSR, Russia, Israel, Switzerland)
12 Ivan Sokolov (Yugoslavia, Bosnia and Herzegovina, Netherlands)
Solution: Cosmopolitans

Photo Connection: pop music
1 H U Karen Carpenter – Karenmeme – Karen Grigoryan/ Asrian
2 I Z Julio Iglesias – Churches (English for Iglesias) – Julio Granda Zuniga
3 D Y Kenny Rogers – Kenny McCormick (South Park) – Ian Rogers
4 F S Eric Clapton – Eric Cartman (South Park) – Eric Hansen
5 A V Billy Joel – Billy the Kid – Joel Lautier
6 E T Robin S – Robin (Batman) – Robin van Kampen

7 G R Luis Fonsi – Luis Suarez –
Luis Engel
8 B W Nana Mouskouri – *Na Na
Hey Hey Kiss them goodbye* – Nana
Dzagnidze
9 C X Harry Styles – Harry
Houdini – Harry Pillsbury

What's the connection? 3
1. Octopus Paul
2. Fine Young Cannibals
3. Mikhail Gorbachev
4. Max Verstappen
5. Samuel Barber
6. Alexander the Great
7. San José
8. Salomon Kalou
9. The Netherlands (according to
https://worldpopulationreview.
com/country-rankings/average-
height-by-country)
10. AVRO 1938. This tournament
was played in ten different cities in
the Netherlands with the following
final standings: 1. Paul Keres 2.
Reuben Fine 3. Mikhail Botwinnik
4. Max Euwe 5. Samuel Reshevsky
6. Alexander Alekhine 7. José Raúl
Capablanca 8. Salomon (Salo) Flohr.

Breaking the rules
Alexandru C.: description 2
Dadang S.: description 4
Evgeniy S.: description 6
Falko B.: description 10
Frederic F.: description 8 (a video
by Frederic Friedel, co-founder of
ChessBase, of the 'cheating', can be
found on YouTube with the title
'World first computer chess cheats')
John von N.: description 1 (using
the name of John von Neumann, a
famous mathematician)
Pier Luigi B.: description 3
Samuel S.: description 7

Sebastien F.: description 5
Tigran P.: description 9

Chess players with glasses
1. Hou Yifan
2. Pentala Harikrishna
3. David Bronstein
4. Matthew Sadler
5. Vladimir Kramnik
6. Fabiano Caruana
7. Max Euwe
8. Artur Kogan
9. Mark Dvoretsky
10. Vasily Smyslov
11. Jeroen van den Berg
12. Robert Hübner
13. Anish Giri
14. Jon Speelman
15. Simen Agdestein
16. Boris Gelfand
Solution: **Near-sightedness**

Two descriptions
1. Chess (Chess was the name of
the Siamese cat of Alekhine. The
famous record company specialised
in blues and R&B is Chess records)
2. Torre (Torre and the Mexican
player Carlos Torre)
3. Anna Rudolf (Anna Rosalie
Rudolf 1865-1940 and Anna Rudolf,
the Hungarian IM and streamer)
4. Feller (Sébastien Feller and Efim
Geller)
5. Dark Horse (the song *Dark Horse*,
the movie *The Dark Horse*)
6. Deep Thought (the computer from
The Hitchhiker's Guide to the Galaxy;
after seven and a half million years of
calculation, the answer finally turns
out to be 42; and IBM named the
chess computer after it)
7. Bronstein (Leon Trotsky was
born as Lev Davidovich Bronstein;
David Bronstein was the youngest

grandmaster when the titles were first awarded in 1950)

8. Lewis (The Lewis Chessmen and the Lewis Gambit)

9. Levon (a song from Elton John's fourth studio album *Madman Across the Water*, the favourite song of Jon Bon Jovi; and Levon Aronian)

10. Swiss Gambit (it is the name of an opening but it is often used in another way. When you start badly in an open tournament but finish higher than you normally would have because of easy pairings, you did a successful Swiss Gambit)

11. Anastasia (Anastasia of Russia, killed at age 17 along with her siblings and parents. She was the inspiration for movies like the 1997 animation movie *Anastasia*; and Anastasia's mate, which got its name from the novel *Anastasia und das Schachspiel*)

12. Martin (Martin is the most common surname in France by a large margin. The English IM Andrew Martin is author of many ChessBase DVD's)

13. MC Hammer (A nice pun by Carlsen and Hammer, named after the rapper, best known for *U Can't Touch This*)

14. Scheveningen (Scheveningen Variation of the Sicilian. The Scheveningen system is a pairing system for a team match in which each player on one team plays each player on the other team)

Solution: coffeehouse game
(for most people that would describe a game in or related to a coffeehouse. For chess players it means a game with bold, often positional unsound play)

What's in a name? 2
1. Jan Timman
2. Jan-Krzysztof Duda
3. John Fedorowicz
4. Yan Nepomniachtchi
5. Jon Ludvig Hammer
6. Dirk Jan ten Geuzendam
7. Jon Speelman
8. Jan Gustafsson
9. Jānis Klovāns
10. Ján Markoš
11. John Nunn
12. Jaan Ehlvest

Solution: John van der Wiel

Logos
1. ChessBase
2. Chessgames.com
3. FollowChess
4. Play Magnus Group
5. Stockfish
6. Norway Chess
7. Magnus Trainer
8. Chess.com
9. Chess24.com
10. *Chess* (the musical)
11. Saint Louis Chess Club
12. ICC (Internet Chess Club)
13. FIDE
14. ECU (European Chess Union)
15. New In Chess
16. Chess Federation of Russia

When they were young 4
1. Maxime Vachier-Lagrave
2. Richárd Rapport
3. Yan Nepomniachtchi
4. Jan-Krzysztof Duda
5. Jon Ludvig Hammer
6. Jorden van Foreest
7. Dmitry Andreikin
8. Fabiano Caruana
9. Hans Niemann
10. Anish Giri
11. Aryan Tari

12. David Howell
Solution: Abhimanyu Mishra
(in 2021 he became the youngest grandmaster ever at 12 years, 4 months and 25 days of age)

Twelve cities
1. Belgrade
2. Havana
3. London
4. Geneva
5. The Hague
6. New York
7. Amsterdam
8. Elista
9. Moscow
10. Chennai
11. Budapest
12. Yerevan
Solution: Buenos Aires

Celeb64: music
1. Frank Sinatra
2. Ennio Morricone
3. Dizzy Gillespie
4. Willie Nelson
5. John Cage
6. Bob Dylan
7. Dmitri Shostakovich
8. Phil Lynott
9. Ringo Starr
10. Jay-Z
11. Andrea Bocelli
12. Sonny & Cher
13. Sting
14. Justin Bieber
15. Bono
Solution: Only a Pawn in Their Game

Who?
1. Fabiano Caruana
2. Barbra Streisand
3. Zurab Azmaiparashvili
4. Jacob Aagaard

5. Jacques Mieses
6. Slim Bouaziz
7. Robert Hübner
8. Friedrich Sämisch
9. Nona Gaprindashvili
10 Géza Maroczy
11 Eric Lobron
12 Alla Kushnir
13 Shakhriyar Mamedyarov
14 Veselin Topalov
Solution: Kasimdzhanov
(Rustam Kasimdzhanov, FIDE world champion in 2004)

Photos: TV series
1. Friends
2. Modern Family
3. The Simpsons
4. Cheers
5. The Wire
6. House
7. The Fresh Prince of Bel–Air
8. Taxi
9. Seinfeld
10. Family Ties
11. The Office US
12. Murder She Wrote
Solution: Beth Harmon

Interviews from New In Chess
Daniil Dubov: quote 10 (in New In Chess magazine 2020-5)
Fabiano Caruana: quote 1 (2018-3)
Gukesh D: quote 3 (2022-6)
Jorden van Foreest: quote 7 (2021-2)
Levon Aronian: quote 2 (2021-3)
Magnus Carlsen: quote 9 (2021-7)
Sam Shankland: quote 5 (2021-5)
Vladimir Kramnik: quote 8 (2019-2, about the Candidates tournament in which he finished second)
Wang Hao: quote 4 (2019-8)
Yan Nepomniachtchi: quote 6 (2022-5)

Fair & Square 3: politicians and others

Arnold Schwarzenegger 9
Aung San Suu Kyi 5
Boris Johnson 1
Donald Trump 6
Elon Musk 3
Johann Wolfgang von Goethe 4
Noam Chomsky 2
Richard Branson 8
Vladimir Putin 7

Photo Connection: sport

1 E Y Michael Jordan – Jordan – Jorden van Foreest
2 B U Serena Williams – F1 Williams – Simon Williams
3 H X Tiger Woods – Anand (Tiger of Madras) – Tiger Hillarp Persson
4 F V Marcell Jacobs (winner 100m 2020 Olympics) – Jacob's Ladder – Jacob Aagaard
5 A S Allyson Felix – Felix the cat – Felix Levin
6 C Z Emil Zátopek (the 'Czech Locomotive') – a Czech Locomotive – Emil Sutovsky
7 D R Sergey Bubka – Sergei Prokofiev – Sergei Movsesian
8 I W Billie Jean King – Larry King – Daniel King
9 G T Muhammad Ali – Ali G – Alireza Firouzja

What's the connection? 4

1. West End Girls
2. Rice
3. Florence
4. Freddie Mercury
5. Andy Murray
6. Bangkok
7. Karpov-Kortchnoi, Baguio 1978; Anatoly Karpov
8. I know

9. ABBA (for the song I Still Have Faith in You)
10. The musical Chess that premiered in London's West End on 14 May 1986. Written by Tim Rice with music by ABBA-members Benny Andersson and Björn Ulvaeus. Inspired by Karpov-Kortchnoi, it is about a match between the Russian grandmaster Anatoly and the American grandmaster Freddy. Anatoly is in love with Florence. Two famous songs in the musical are One Night in Bangkok by Murray Head and I Know Him So Well.

When they were young 5

1. Sergei Tiviakov
2. Jeroen Piket
3. Eric Lobron
4. Yasser Seirawan
5. Boris Gelfand
6. Evgeny Bareev
7. Matthew Sadler
8. Liviu-Dieter Nisipeanu
9. Vladimir Akopian
10. Dimitri Reinderman
11. Gata Kamsky
12. Michael Adams
Solution: Predecessors

Guess and refute the blunders

1. In **Steinitz**-Voigt, White probably didn't feel any danger after the weak moves of his opponent, let alone expected to be mated next move. And yet, that is what happened: 12.0-0 ♛xh2.
2. Bird-**Lasker 12.♘e6#**
3. Wiersma-**Euwe 10.♘xf6+** winning a rook after 10...gxf6 11.♛xd8+ ♚xd8 12.♗xf6.
4. Kortchnoi-**Spassky 12.♘d5** 1-0 Maybe Black missed that 12...♚d8 prevents losing a piece, though the

position is still lost. 'It is said that after the game, the 11-years-old Spassky left the tournament hall in tears' (according to Megabase).

5. **Petrosian**-Ree **8.♕b3** Black loses a piece. In the six other database games with this position, Black still played on. Five players lost, but one player won against a 2320 player!

6. Zapata-**Anand.** There are 70 games in the database with this position, in 32 White played **6.♕e2**, just like Zapata did. After 6...♕e7 7.♘d5 ♕d7 8.d3 White wins a piece. In the prearranged draw Miles-Christiansen White took on e4. The story goes that before doing that, he polished the e2-square with his finger to make his opponent nervous... Another story is that Anand knew about this game, but according to Stewart Reuben on an English chess forum Anand told him he wasn't aware of that game when he blundered.

7. Christiansen-**Karpov 12.♕d1** with a double attack on ♗d6 and ♘h5. In 1993, the Wijk aan Zee tournament had moved away from the traditional round-robin format and went for knockout matches. Despite the knockout blow delivered this game, Karpov won the match and later the tournament. Christiansen moved on to the open tournament but did badly there, finishing in the bottom.

8. Willemze-**Gaprindashvili 11.♕e1** attacks the two unprotected black knights on b4 and e4.

9. **Hou**-Lalith **5...hxg4.** This is the shortest loss by a grandmaster (apart from losses by default etc.). This was in round 10: in the previous nine rounds Hou Yifan was paired with seven female players. She suspected this was intentional (without having any proof) and the quick loss was her way of protesting against it.

10. Ding-**Carlsen 4.♕xd2.** In the semi-final of the online Chessable Masters tournament, Liren Ding disconnected in his first match game (of four) against Magnus Carlsen and lost on time in a drawn rook endgame. The World Champion didn't want to win the match because of this and decided to return the point in the second match game.

11. Mamedyarov-**Kasparov 7.0-0.** Kasparov retired from classical chess in 2005, but still plays the occasional rapid or blitz tournament. Zagreb blitz 2021 was a disaster for him though: 0.5/9, often struggling already in the opening. Against Mamedyarov he blundered with 5...♘f6 and in the final position Black is totally lost with ♘g5 of exd4 and ♖e1 coming.

Celeb64: others

1. Leo Tolstoy
2. Peter Thiel (rated 2199! See https://ratings.fide.com/ profile/2022389)
3. Bill Gates
4. Menachem Begin
5. Bertolt Brecht
6. George Bernard Shaw
7. Benjamin Franklin
8. Diana Spencer
9. Fidel Castro
10. Che Guevara
11. Marcel Duchamp
12. Vladimir Nabokov
13. Man Ray

14. Richard Branson
15. Carmen Kass
Solution: Amateur players

Tweets
1. Garry Kasparov
2. Anish Giri
3. Anna Rudolf
4. Susan Polgar
5. Magnus Carlsen
6. Teimour Radjabov
7. Sergey Karjakin
8. Nigel Short
9. Judit Polgar
10. Hikaru Nakamura

Women's World Champions
1. Xie Jun
2. Zhu Chen (married to Qatari grandmaster Mohammed Al-Modiahki)
3. Maia Chiburdanidze (January 1988, 48th with 2560)
4. Hou Yifan (Wikipedia: 'In 2020, at age 26, Hou became the youngest ever professor at Shenzhen University where she is a professor at the School of Physical Education, which includes chess in its Sports Training Program')
5. Antoaneta Stefanova (she is a member of Parliament for the populist political party There Is Such a People and was even nominated as the party's candidate for the prime minister position)
6. Nona Gaprindashvili (in *The Queen's Gambit* it was incorrectly stated that Gaprindashvili is Russian and never played competitive chess against men. She took offense to that).
7. Alexandra Kosteniuk (see https://www.imdb.com/name/nm1445717/)
8. Lyudmila Rudenko (Wikipedia: 'At age 10, Rudenko was taught how to play chess by her father – although, at first, she was more interested in swimming. After secondary school, she moved to Odessa and took a degree in economics. Rudenko became the swimming champion of Odessa in the 400-metre (1,300 ft) breaststroke. In 1925, she was swimming vice-champion of Ukraine (breaststroke).'
9. Susan Polgar (to be exact, Wikipedia again: 'Her title defence against Xie Jun of China was scheduled to take place in 1998 but FIDE had been unable to find a satisfactory sponsor. In early 1999, a match was arranged, but under conditions to which Polgar objected. As a result, Polgar requested a postponement because she was pregnant and due to give birth to a child, Tom, in March 1999. She felt that she did not have sufficient time to recuperate, and secondly because the match was to be held entirely in China, the home country of her challenger. She also wanted a larger prize fund matching at least the minimum stipulated by FIDE regulations at the time (200000 CHF).
When Polgar refused to play under these conditions, FIDE declared that she had forfeited the title.'
10. Vera Menchik (strong players who lost against Menchik were said to be members of the Vera Menchik Club. Euwe had only +1 -2 =1 against her and so he was declared the president of the club.
11. Mariya Muzychuk (the 2017 Women's World Chess

Championship was held in Iran. Mariya Muzychuk refused to participate out of protest of being obligated to wear a hijab. Sister Anna Muzychuk did play the tournament. She made it to the finals but lost to Tan Zhongyi)
Solution: Judit Polgar

Photos: movies
1. *The Addams Family*
2. *Casablanca*
3. *The Seventh Seal*
4. *Aladdin*
5. *Naked Gun 33⅓: The Final Insult*
6. *Spice World*
7. *Austin Powers: The Spy Who Shagged Me*
8. *Pretty Woman*
9. *2001 A Space Odyssey*
10. *The Big Lebowski*
11. *Ray*
12. *X-Men 2* (also known as *X2: X-Men United* or just *X2*)
Solution: From Russia with Love

What's in a name? 3
1. Miguel Najdorf
2. Mikhail Gurevich
3. Mikhail Botvinnik
4. Mikhail Tal
5. Michael Basman
6. Mike Klein
7. Adrian Mikhalchishin
8. Mihail Marin
9. Mikhail Chigorin
10. Michael Adams
11. Miguel Quinteros
12. Michal Krasenkow
Solution: Miguel Illescas

Celeb64: sports
1. Manny Pacquiao
2. Daniil Medvedev
3. Usain Bolt
4. Novak Djokovic
5. Lennox Lewis
6. Boris Becker
7. Steve Davis
8. Mohamed Salah
9. Kobe Bryant
10. Wilt Chamberlain
11. Pep Guardiola
12. Mick Schumacher
13. Kareem Abdul-Jabbar
14. Vitaly Klitschko
15. Osvaldo Ardiles
Solution: Simen Agdestein
(the Norwegian football international (8 caps) who was also pretty decent in chess)

Ranking the Stars: Megabase games
1. Nakamura
2. Kortchnoi
3. Shirov
4. Farago
5. Ivanchuk
6. Grischuk
7. Carlsen
8. Van Wely
9. Kamsky
10. Aronian
Solution: TWIC archive

Photo Connection: cities
1 I U San Sebastian – Sebastian Vettel – Sebastian Siebrecht
2 B Y Frankfurt – Swiss franc – Frank Marshall
3 E T St. Louis – Louis Vuitton – Louis Paulsen
4 C X Sofia – Hagia Sophia – Sofia Polgar
5 H Z Johannesburg – Johan Cruijff – Johann Hjartarson
6 D R Saint Petersburg – Peter Rabbit – Peter Heine Nielsen

7 G W Yekaterinburg – Catherine Zeta-Jones – Kateryna Lagno
8 F S Milan – Milan Kundera – Milan Vidmar
9 A V San Francisco – Francisco Franco – Francisco Vallejo Pons

What's the connection? 5

1. Bird (Charlie 'Bird' Parker)
2. *Norwegian Wood*
3. Vasily Smyslov
4. (Republic of) the Marshall Islands
5. Anatoly Karpov
6. C30, C60, C90, Go! (or C'30 C'60 C'90 Go)
7. Irving Berlin
8. Mikhail Chigorin
9. The Spanish Inquisition (in a series of sketches in *Monty Python's Flying Circus*, Series 2 Episode 2)
10. The Ruy Lopez (or Spanish Opening). 1, 2, 3, 4, 5, 7 and 8 refer to variations of this opening, 6 to the ECO code C60 to C99.

When they were young 6

1. Teimour Radjabov
2. Luke McShane
3. Baadur Jobava
4. Alejandro Ramirez
5. Étienne Bacrot
6. Gawain Jones
7. David Smerdon
8. Ivan Cheparinov
9. Erwin l'Ami
10. Francisco Vallejo Pons
11. Alexander Grischuk
12. Arkadij Naiditsch

Solution: Avoiding preparation

Leftovers

1. The opponents of Anderssen were Lionel Kieseritzky (Immortal Game) and Jean Dufresne (Evergreen Game).
2. Neither of them received the grandmaster title, as they were all dead when the titles were first rewarded in 1950.
3. At the last minute, a commanding officer asked to see the list of prisoner names and recognized Bernstein's name as he was a chess enthusiast. After confronting Bernstein about his identity, the commanding officer offered him a deal he couldn't refuse.: they would play a game of chess. If Bernstein won the game, he would win his life and freedom. However, if he drew or lost, he would get shot along with the rest of the prisoners. Bernstein won in short order and was released.
4. Badminton.
5. The Soviet delegation missed a player. Because there had to be an even number of participants, Lodewijk Prins was excluded from the tournament. He filed a lawsuit against Staunton and was awarded 3000 guilders compensation, which would be about 40,000 euro now.
6. Vytautas Landsbergis.
7. Fischer's proposal was the first player to win ten games to win the match with no limit to the length of the match. That was accepted. He also wanted the defending champion to keep his title in case of the score being nine wins to nine wins. That was refused.
8. The Philippine grandmaster Rosendo Balinas.
9. Kortchnoi wanted to check if short castling was allowed. 'In the two and a half thousand games that I had played, there had never

been an instance where it had been necessary for me to castle when my rook was attacked, and I was not sure that I understood correctly the rules of the game!'

10. Lubomir Kavalek (who was friends with Forman).

11. Habu is one of the best Shogi players ever. He still occasionally plays a chess tournament. His highest FIDE rating has been 2415.

12. She is the widow of Bobby Fischer. A court has ruled that they married in 2004.

13. The winner, Alexander Georgiev, is a ten-time world champion in draughts.

14. The Double Bongcloud, famous because of the game Carlsen-Nakamura, played in the Magnus Carlsen Invitational on March 15, 2021.

15. He tested positive for the corona virus in a PCR test before the eleventh round, meaning he couldn't play the last three rounds.

16. Monaco. They have three grandmasters with a population of close to 40,000. Iceland is number two with fourteen grandmasters, population about 376,000.

17A Misha Osipov, 3 years old, is crying after losing to Anatoly Karpov on Russian television. Karpov had offered him a draw, but he refused.

17B Timur Gareyev is concentrating on his bike during his world record 48-board blind simul in 2016.

17C Carlsen has been thrown in the swimming pool after winning the 2013 World Championships against Vishy Anand.

17D Inarkiev had made an illegal move against Carlsen: he left himself in check while giving a check. Carlsen didn't claim but made a king move, ♔d3. According to Inarkiev, this was illegal, and he claimed a win. An arbiter did give him a point but was overruled by the chief arbiter and Carlsen got the win.

17E Fabiano Caruana does the ice bucket challenge. This challenge was started in 2014 to promote awareness of the disease ALS.

17F Ivanchuk was called to the stage for winning the 2016 rapid world championship while playing a checkers game with Jobava. On the podium after receiving the gold medal he was still calculating variations. He then quickly returned to the game, winning with a nice combination.

Image sources

Preface
A. Wikimedia/Mathias Appel
B. Wikimedia/Thomas Steffan
Y. Wikimedia/Public domain
Z. Wikimedia/Public domain

When they were young 1
1. NIC Archive
2. Jac. de Nijs/Nationaal Archief
4. NIC Archive
5. NIC Archive
7. Turov Archive
8. Turov Archive
10. Collection David DeLucia
12. NIC Archive

Chess players and their eyes
1. Lennart Ootes
2. Dirk Jan ten Geuzendam
3. Dirk Jan ten Geuzendam
4. Dirk Jan ten Geuzendam
5. Dirk Jan ten Geuzendam
6. NIC Archive
7. Lennart Ootes
8. NIC Archive
9. Dirk Jan ten Geuzendam
10. Joris van Velzen
11. Lennart Ootes
12. Dirk Jan ten Geuzendam
13. Lennart Ootes
14. NIC Archive

Photo Connection: countries
B. Universal Pictures
D. Nail Polish: Ralf Roletschek / Roletschek.at
F. Austrian Airlines
G. Andreas Tille/Wikimedia
I. Wikipedia
R. Dirk Jan ten Geuzendam

S. Dirk Jan ten Geuzendam
T. NIC Archive
U. Dirk Jan ten Geuzendam
V. Dirk Jan ten Geuzendam
W. Dirk Jan ten Geuzendam
X. Dirk Jan ten Geuzendam
Y. Les Deux Guitares (Barclay)
Z. NIC Archive

Celeb64: movies
1. Orion Pictures
5. 20th Television
6. Public domain
8. Metro-Goldwyn-Mayer
11. Colombia Pictures
13. Metro-Goldwyn-Mayer
14. bobbydarin.net
15. Sony/Colombia Pictures Industries Inc.

When they were young 2
1. Cathy Rogers
3. Cathy Rogers
4. Cathy Rogers
5. Cathy Rogers
7. Cathy Rogers
8. Cathy Rogers
9. Cathy Rogers
10. Cathy Rogers
11. Cathy Rogers
12. Cathy Rogers

Chess players with a beard and/or a moustache
1. Dirk Jan ten Geuzendam
2. Gerard de Graaf
3. René Olthof
4. Lennart Ootes
5. Dirk Jan ten Geuzendam
6. Lennart Ootes
7. Lennart Ootes
8. Lennart Ootes
9. NIC Archive
10. NIC Archive

11. Dirk Jan ten Geuzendam
12. Dirk Jan ten Geuzendam
13. René Olthof
14. NIC Archive
15. Bundesarchiv, Bild 102-00457 / CC-BY-SA 3.0
16. Lennart Ootes

Photo Connection: political leaders
1. Ben Shread / Cabinet Office
6. CC-BY-4.0: © European Union 2022
8. European People's Party
C. Wikimedia/NordNordWest
F. Glen Thomas
I. Wikimedia /Saltmarsh
R. Dirk Jan ten Geuzendam
S. Dirk Jan ten Geuzendam
T. NIC Archive
U. NIC Archive
V. NIC Archive
W. Bundesarchiv, Bild 102-00457 / CC-BY-SA 3.0
X. Dirk Jan ten Geuzendam
Y. René Olthof
Z. Dirk Jan ten Geuzendam

Celeb64: movies and TV
1. Image Entertainment
3. NBC
4. Epix
6. Fox Studio
7. Sony Pictures
9. Planet Chess
11. Image Entertainment
14. Fox

Photo Connection: pop music
2. Dr. Ueli Frey, http://www.drjazz.ch
3. Wikimedia /Nicolas Lacoste
5. Wikimedia/David Shankbone
6. Ron Kroon for Anefo
7. Wikimedia/Sheila Herman
9. Wikimedia /Lovclyhes

D Wikipedia/Comedy Central Press
E Batman Wiki
F Wikipedia/Comedy Central Press
G Wikimedia /Ailura
I Fr. Longenecker
S Lennart Ootes
T René Olthof
U Dirk Jan ten Geuzendam
V NIC Archive
W Dirk Jan ten Geuzendam
X NIC Archive
Y René Olthof
Z Dirk Jan ten Geuzendam

When they were young 3
1. Jerome Bibuld
2. Cathy Rogers
3. Cathy Rogers
4. Cathy Rogers
5. Cathy Rogers
6. Rainer Knaak
7. Cathy Rogers
9. Cathy Rogers
10. Diana Matisone
11. Cathy Rogers

Chess players with glasses
1. Lennart Ootes
2. Dirk Jan ten Geuzendam
3. NIC Archive
4. Dirk Jan ten Geuzendam
5. Lennart Ootes
6. Dirk Jan ten Geuzendam
7. NIC Archive
8. Dirk Jan ten Geuzendam
9. NIC Archive
10. Gerard de Graaf
11. Dirk Jan ten Geuzendam
12. NIC Archive
13. Dirk Jan ten Geuzendam
14. Gerard de Graaf

15. Dirk Jan ten Geuzendam
16. Dirk Jan ten Geuzendam

When they were young 4
1. NIC Archive
2. René Olthof
3. Cathy Rogers
4. NIC Archive
5. Cathy Rogers
6. Frans Peeters
7. Cathy Rogers
9. Judith van Amerongen
10. anishgiriofficial.com
11. Cathy Rogers

Celeb64: music
5. John Cage Trust
6. Daniel Kramer
11. FIDE
14. Justin Bieber

Photos: TV series
1. Warner Bros. Television
2. 20th Television
3. 20th Television
4. CBS Television
5. HBO Enterprises
6. NBCUniversal Television
7. Warner Bros. Television
8. Paramount Television
9. Columbia Pictures Television
10. Paramount Television
11. NBCUniversal Television
12. NBCUniversal Television

Photo Connection: sport
2. Wikimedia/Vinod Divakaran
4. www.governo.it
5. Wikimedia/Eckhard Pecher
7. Wikimedia/Vinod Divakaran
8. Wikimedia/Lynn Gilbert

9. Wikimedia/John Mathew Smith
B. Wikimedia/Jenn Ross/\
C. FUNET railway pictures archive funet.fi
E. Wikipedia/Vardion
G. Wikimedia/Sj
H. Ten Geuzendam
I. Wikimedia/Gage Skidmore

When they were young 5
1. Archive Postovsky
2. J. Piket
3. Wikimedia/Gerhard Hund
6. Archive Postovsky
7. Archive Jacoby
9. Archive Postovsky
10. Maja Reinderman

Celeb64: others
2. FIDE
3. Monkberry
5. Bertolt Brecht archive
8. Alamy
14. Richard Branson

Photos: movies
1. Paramount Pictures
2. Warner Bros. Pictures
3. AB Svensk Filmindustri
4. Walt Disney Pictures
5. Paramount Pictures
6. Icon Entertainment International
7. New Line Cinema
8. Buena Vista Pictures
9. Metro-Goldwyn-Mayer
10. PolyGram Filmed Entertainment
11. Universal Pictures
12. 20th Century Fox

Celeb64: sport
1. facebook.com/MannyPacquiao
2. UTS
3. Instagram Usain Bolt

4. facebook.com/djokovic.official
5. BBC
6. Lennart Ootes
7. Batsford
9. NBA
11. Bleacher Report UK
12. Haas F1 Team
13. Iconomy LLC
14. KMG/Klitschko press service

Photo Connection: cities
2. rupp.de/Wikimedia
3. Ten Geuzendam
8. Paolo da Reggio/Wikimedia
C. Arild Vågen/Wikimedia
E. Louis Vutton/Wikimedia
G. David Shankbone/Wikimedia
I. Sebastian Vettel: Morio/Wikimedia
R. René Olthof
S. NIC Archive
T. NIC Archive
U. René Olthof
V. NIC Archive
W. Dirk Jan ten Geuzendam
X. NIC Archive
Y. Public domain
Z. Dirk Jan ten Geuzendam

When they were young 6
3. Cathy Rogers
4. NIC Archive
6. Cathy Rogers
7. Cathy Rogers
9. erwinlami.nl
11. Gerhard Hund/Wikimedia
12. Arkadij Naiditsch

Leftovers
B Lennart Ootes
E Lennart Ootes
F Lennart Ootes